Doug Moench Chuck Dixon

writers

Jim Aparo Norm Breyfogle
Graham Nolan Jim Balent

pencillers

Scott Hanna Norm Breyfogle
Jim Aparo Tom Mandrake
Bob Wiacek Joe Rubinstein
Dick Giordano

inkers

Adrienne Roy

colorist

Richard Starkings John Costanza
Tim Harkins

letterers

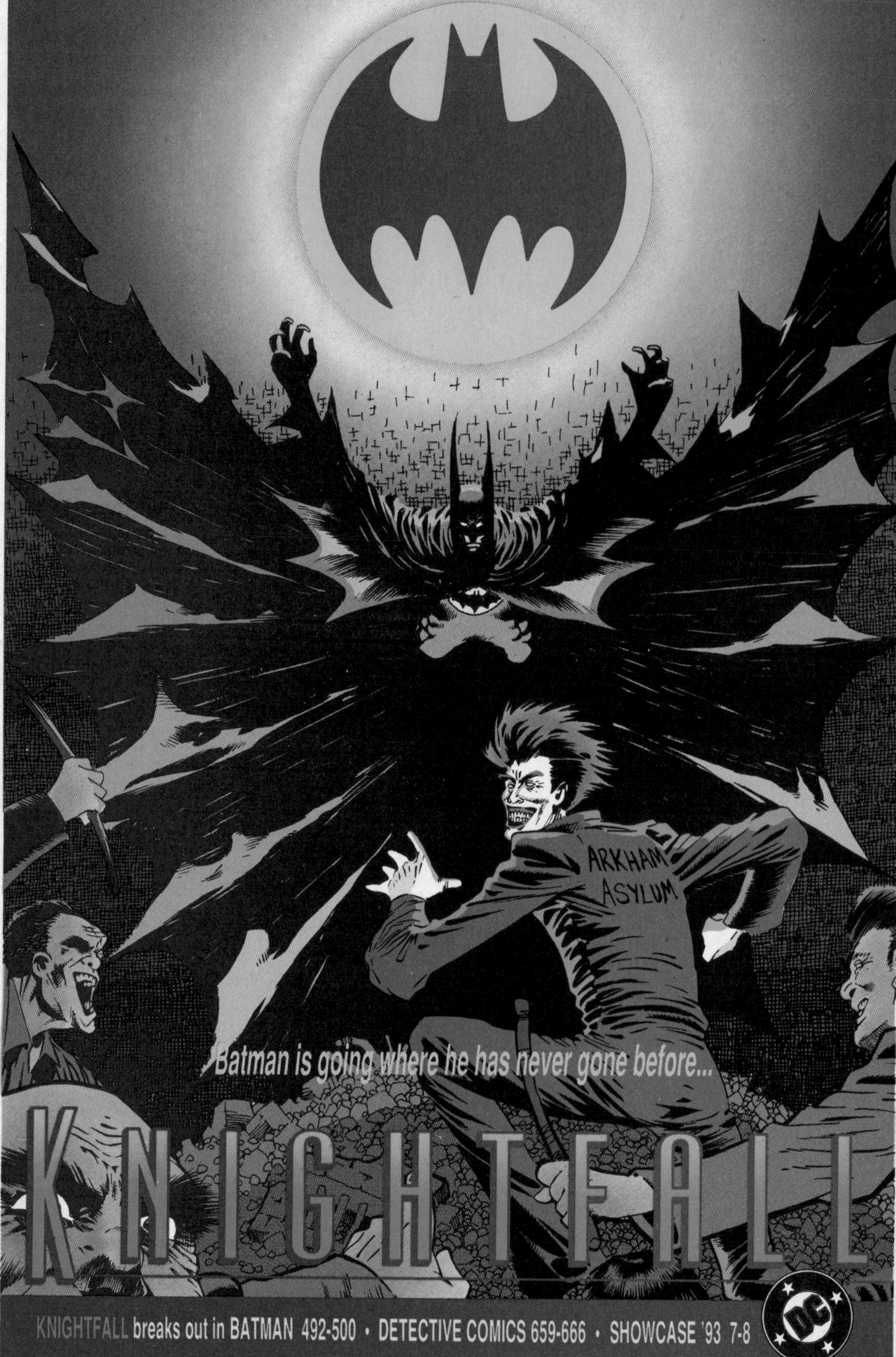

ARKHAM
ASYLUM
Batman is going where he has never gone before...
KNIGHTFALL
KNIGHTFALL breaks out in BATMAN 492-500 • DETECTIVE COMICS 659-666 • SHOWCASE '93 7-8
DC

VRRRRRRRRR

HEY, WHAT'S THAT--?

OVER THERE!

PETERSON

I DON'T KNOW, MAN... BUT IT'S COMIN' THIS WAY...

RRRRRRR

HALT!

RRRR

IDENTIFY YOURSELF!

RRR

1

THE Freedom OF MADNESS!
OPEN FIRE!
BRAM BRAM
BRAM
BRAM BRAM
SPANG
CHEEOW
ZANG
ZING
RRRRRRRRRRRR
BATMAN CREATED BY BOB KANE
DOUG MOENCH WRITER
JIM APARO ARTIST
ADRIENNE ROY COLORIST
RICHARD STARKINGS LETTERER
SCOTT PETERSON JORDAN B. GORFINKEL ASSISTANT EDITORS
DENNY O'NEIL EDITOR
2

BRAM BRAM
CBEK
SHREEEEEEE
ZING
SPAK
RUNNN!
43RD ARMO
YAAAH
BUMP
RRRRRRRRRRRRRR
TIME TO GO --
TEK
3

BA-OOMM
VRMM
SKREECH
FIVE MINUTES MAXIMUM...
LOAD ALL THE WEAPON CRATES YOU CAN...
... BUT DON'T FORGET THE STINGERS.
4

POLICE H.Q:
IT'S LIKE AN ORDNANCE INVENTORY FOR WORLD WAR THREE, COMMISH...

AUTOMATIC ASSAULT RIFLES, ANTI-PERSONNEL MINES, MORTARS, HEAVY MACHINEGUNS, FRAGMENTATION GRENADES...
PIZZA KITCHEN
...AN' EVEN A FEW CRATES O' SHOULDER-LAUNCHED STINGER MISSILES.

AND THE ONLY BRIGHT SIDE IS THAT NO ONE WAS HURT...
NOT AFTER THE ARMORY GUARDS RAN AWAY FROM THEIR U.F.O MONSTER... BUT SOMETHING TELLS ME THERE'S STILL A BODY COUNT TO COME.

THEN YOU THINK THOSE MUNITIONS WERE STOLEN FOR DOMESTIC USE, MONTOYA?
WITH THAT M.O, COMMISSIONER, I DON'T KNOW WHAT TO THINK...

MY GUESS IS NICARAGUA -- ROGUE C.I.A ELEMENTS.

...BUT ONE THING'S READY FOR THE BANK -- THAT WAS A WHOLE TRUCKLOAD OF MIGHTY EXOTIC WEAPONRY...
...AND RIGHT NOW IT'S LOOSE ON OUR STREETS!

YES...
...BUT IN WHOSE HANDS?
5

WE START BY HITTING THE VIOLENT WARDS HERE AT THE CENTER OF THE ROUNDHOUSE...

THE FIRST HIT WILL BE RELATIVELY LIGHT, JUST ENOUGH TO BREACH THE ROOF AND A FEW OF THE CELLS -- BUT THE SECOND HIT WILL BE HEAVY, TAKING OUT SECURITY AND SEALING THE CORRIDOR BETWEEN ADMINISTRATION AND INMATES.

... AND WE FOLLOW WITH A HIT ON MAIN SECURITY -- HERE.

WE'VE CERTAINLY GOT THE FIREPOWER FOR IT.

BUT WHICH CELL DO WE OPEN FIRST? WHO CAN LEAD THE OTHERS -- INSPIRE THEM WITH HIS OWN VIOLENCE AND MADNESS?

I THINK I MAY HAVE A SUGGESTION, BANE...

AND BELIEVE ME, HE'S A REAL RIOT!
ARKHAM ASYLUM
NORTH
ELEVATION
The incessant laughter alone, echoing through dark steel corridors, is enough to make one doubt the very existence of sanity...

Add to that all the shrieks and whimpers, the snarls and whispers, all the cunning drool-garbled incantations of paranoia and revenge, and one sees that this is NOT, in fact, an ASYLUM.
It is, simply and unarguably, a MADHOUSE.
ARKHAM ASYLUM FOR THE CRIMINALLY INSANE
NOT, in fact, an ASYLUM.
It is simply and unarguably, a MADHOUSE.
And if one is the keeper and controller of such a place, does that make one SANE -- or merely the KING of the MAD?
Indeed, one won
to
eks and
spers, all the
incantations
nd one sees
Indeed, one wonders if madness might not be INFECTIOUS in a certain sense, a contagion by virtue of its omnipresent influence, so much more vivid and strident than the mundane, smothering cloak of so-called normalcy.
If so, then surely I have been infected by now, for the laughter and shrieks, the canny gasps from the gloom, are the voices with which I live, here in Arkham, here in the madhouse of my making.
They have become my world, echoing down steel corridors to enter my MIND -- where they echo, now, even LOUDER...
...clamoring to get out.
REAL SHORT?
I WANT IT OFF -- OUT OF THE WAY.
YOU GOT IT.
NO, I DON'T, NOT YET. BUT I WILL GET IT.
SHKKT
7

Y'KNOW, YOU'RE GETTIN' TOO INTENSE FOR ME, JEAN PAUL, ACTIN' LIKE YOU DON'T EVEN NEED YOUR SPECS ANY--
CON-TACTS WORK BETTER, ALL RIGHT? LESS TO WORRY ABOUT.

YEAH, SURE, NO NEED TO GET SO--
JUST CUT THE HAIR, ROBIN, SO WE CAN GET ON WITH MY WORKOUT, Huh? AFTER WHAT KILLER CROC DID TO ME, IT'S TIME TO GET TOUGH.
YOU'RE CERTAIN THAT'S HIS CELL?
POSITIVE, BANE -- THIRD UNIT IN THE VIOLENT WARD...

GOT IT FROM THE SAME FORMER GUARD WE PAID OFF TO ACQUIRE THE BLUEPRINTS... AND EVEN IF THE SHOT'S NOT PERFECT, YOU'RE BOUND TO BREACH ONE OF THE VIOLENT CELLS.
I'LL MAKE IT PERFECT.

NITRO'S READY.
NOW, BANE.
KRAK
8

BAMM
BAOUMM
WHAT THE--?!
ORDERLIES!
THE SKY...
...IS... FALLING..?
YESSS...
YES!
HA HA HA HA HA HA HA HA
HURRY!
9

HELLO, GUARD...
CHOOM
...GOODBYE, MEAT!

ZOOSH

KROOM

LAUNDRY

OPEN SEZ *ME*-- BECAUSE IT'S TIME FOR THE *INMATES* TO RUN THIS ASYLUM!
HAHAHAHAHA
OPEN
CLOSE

BESIDES, WE MAY NEED THE SPACE FOR A *NEW* PATIENT.
VMMMM

FREE! YOU'RE ALL FREE!
CHOOM
HAHAHAHAHA
OKAY, BANE -- ZOMBIE AND TROGG ARE LIFTING OFF IN THE CHOPPER.
WHP WHP WHP
ZOOSH
KAKROOM
GREETINGS, JEREMIAH ARKHAM -- AND WELCOME TO THE MAD-HOUSE!
YOUR CELL AWAITS!
HAHA HA HA HAHA
11

THEY'RE COMING OUT INTO THE YARD, TROGG...
DROP THE PRESENTS.
CRATES GOING OUT NOW.
FWUFF
GUNNNNS!
KRATCH
ZOMBIE TO BANE: PRESENTS DELIVERED...
...BUT THE STATE POLICE HAVE ARRIVED -- ENTERING THE GROUNDS NOW...
"STILL, IT SHOULD BE A FAIR FIGHT NOW."
STATE POLICE
IT'LL BE MORE THAN FAIR, ZOMBIE...
12

"... FAR MORE THAN FAIR."
MY GOD! WH-WHAT... WHAT'S HAPPENING OUT THERE?
BRAM BRAM BRAM BRAM
BRAKAKAK

SOMEONE REGARDS YOUR NEW SECURITY WITH CONTEMPT, JEREMIAH ARKHAM: SOMEONE FINDS AMUSEMENT IN THE NOTION OF MADNESS BOILING AND SCAMPERING FROM THESE WALLS.
BUT NOW... SHALL WE TALK?
HA HA HA HA HA HA HA HA

HE AIN'T SHOWN YET, Huh, COMMISH?
NOT YET, BULLOCK -- BUT YOU SENT THE TACTICAL UNITS TO BACK UP THE STATE POLICE?
ON THEIR WAY...

AND OUR NEW MAYOR UNFORTUNATELY REQUESTS YOUR PLEASURE -- AT HIS MANSION -- NOW.
FIGURES -- PROBABLY ABOUT THE ARMORY THEFT... ALL THOSE WEAPONS IN THE HANDS OF LUNATICS.
IT SURE AIN'T ABOUT THE NEW COLOR SCHEME FOR HIS OFFICE!

ALL RIGHT... SHUT OFF THE SIGNAL, BULLOCK.
GIVIN' UP ON THE BATMAN, COMMISH?
WITH ANY LUCK, HE'S ALREADY HEARD ABOUT THE ARKHAM RIOT -- HALFWAY THERE BY NOW.

... SEVENTY-EIGHT... SEVENTY-NINE...
THE BATSIGNAL -- BUT IT JUST WENT OUT.
I WONDER WHAT--
DEET DEET DEET
13

...EIGHTY-TWO... EIGHTY-THREE...
ROBIN HERE. WHAT'S--
I'M UPSTATE-- ALMOST AT ARKHAM. YOU STAY IN GOTHAM.
ARKHAM? BUT... IF YOU'RE STILL SICK -- SO OUT OF IT YOU CAN BARELY GET OUT OF BED...

...MAYBE YOU SHOULD HAVE SOME HEL--
OVER AND OUT.

MORE PUSHUPS--
YEAH-- AND YET ANOTHER PUT-DOWN.

BRAKAKAKAKAKA
CHOOM
SPANG
SPANG
SO WHEN DO WE GET TO RETURN FIRE?
MAYBE NEVER -- AS LONG AS THEY'VE GOT HOSTAGES IN THERE.

IN PLACE OF OUR *MADNESS*, JEREMIAH, YOU GAVE US *RESTRAINT* AND CALLED IT A PRODUCT OF *YOUR SANITY*.

BUT HOW SANE DO YOU FEEL *NOW*, JEREMIAH -- NOW THAT *YOU'RE* RESTRAINED?

HA HA HA HA HAHA HA

WHAT'S *THAT*?
JUST A *BAT*...
BIGGEST BAT *I* EVER SAW -- MORE LIKE THE BAT-*MAN*...

"YOU *CRAZY*? HE CAN'T *FLY*--!"

HE'S *HERE*... BUT HE'LL NEVER *STOP* THEM.
DON'T BE SO *SURE*, BANE. I'VE SEEN THE BATMAN PULL OFF SOME MIGHTY --
YOUR GOTHAM EXPERTISE IS *APPRECIATED*, BIRD...

... BUT I *KNOW* THIS MAN ... I HAVE BEEN *CLOSE* TO HIM.
I HAVE *SMELLED* WHAT HE IS...
15

"EVEN IF HE COULD STOP THEM, HE WON'T.
"HE WILL CHOOSE THE SAVING OF LIVES OVER THE APPREHENSION OF KILLERS...
DEAD.
"HE ALWAYS DOES.
"AND AS FOR THE POLICE... THEY NEVER HAD A CHANCE."
HEY-- IT'S THE CAVALRY!
STATE POLICE
STATE POLICE
ABOUT TIME!
WHAT'S THE CURRENT HOSTAGE SITUATION?
MOST OF THE ORDERLIES HAVE MANAGED TO HOLE UP IN THE ROUNDHOUSE GARRISON -- BUT, BEFORE THE 'PHONE LINES WERE CUT, THEY REPORTED A NUMBER OF GUARDS DOWN...
...AND JEREMIAH ARKHAM TAKEN BY THE JOKER.
THE JOKER--?
"--THEN GOD HELP HIM."
ALL YOUR NEW SECURITY, JEREMIAH, BREACHED LIKE A WET PAPER BAG... ALL YOUR HARD WORK, UNDONE IN A TWINKLING OF FRENZY.
I LIKE THE WORD "TWINKLING," DON'T YOU? WERE YOU HARD TO POTTY TRAIN, JEREMIAH?
DOESN'T MATTER -- BECAUSE EVERYTHING YOU'VE TRAINED FOR, EVERYTHING YOU'VE ACCOMPLISHED, IS SHATTERED...
...JUST LIKE YOUR MIND RIGHT NOW, JEREMIAH -- SHATTERED.
HAHAHA
16

OW'D THEY GET
OUT INTO THE YARD?
WHAT HAPPENED
TO THE WALL?
NEAR AS WE CAN FIGURE... SOME KIND OF SMART MISSILES.
MISSILES? BUT WHO THE--?

"WE DON'T KNOW... BUT OBVIOUSLY SOMEONE A LOT BETTER EQUIPPED THAN SADDAM HUSSEIN."
RAKA
CHOOM
BLAM BLAM

--ALREADY DISPATCHED FIVE OF OUR TACTICAL UNITS, MR. MAYOR, TO ASSIST THE STATE POLICE ON THE SCENE...

... BUT WITH THE HOSTAGE SITUATION, I DON'T KNOW WHAT ANY COP COULD --
I CERTAINLY HOPE THEY'VE BEEN TOLD TO SHOOT TO KILL.

IT DOESN'T WORK THAT WAY, MAYOR KROL. MY MEN DISCHARGE THEIR FIREARMS ONLY TO DEFEND THEMSELVES -- OR OTHERS.

THEN YOU'RE GOING TO HAVE A LOT OF DEAD MEN, GORDON -- SOMETHING I DO NOT WANT DURING MY ADMINISTRATION.
I RAN ON A LAW AND ORDER PLATFORM -- AND NOW THAT I'VE BEEN ELECTED, I'M NOT ABOUT TO ABANDON EVERYTHING I STAND FOR.

YOU RAN UNOPPOSED.
EVEN MORE PROOF OF MY MANDATE!
PROOF OF YOUR MACHINE...
17

"... AND THAT'S WHAT WE NEED NOW -- NOT A FIREFIGHT, BUT ONE MAN, ON THE INSIDE, FUNCTIONING LIKE A MACHINE."
THEY'RE COMING... THEY'VE GOT CONTROL OF THE LOCKDOWN STATION... NO WAY TO KEEP THEM OUT...
MY GOD, THEY HATE US... WE'RE DEAD... WE'RE FRIGGIN' --
WHAT THE--?
PHOOM
WOK
CHAT
CHOOF
WAKK
18

TAKE THE WEAPONS AND STAY HERE.
I'LL LOCK YOU IN.
YOU BEEFED UP SECURITY AND WHAT DID YOU GET, HAH? THE BEEFIEST BREAKOUT OF MADNESS IN ARKHAM'S HISTORY!
AND SOON YOUR OWN MADNESS WILL BREAK OUT, JEREMIAH, RIGHT OUT OF YOUR SHATTERED SKULL -- JUST AS SOON AS THOSE KNEES WEAKEN!
"BUT YOU'LL ENJOY THE FREEDOM OF MADNESS, JEREMIAH!"
TRUST ME! MADNESS IS THE ONLY FREEDOM --AND ALL THE MADNESS ONCE RESTRAINED UNDER YOUR STRICT CONTROL WILL SOON BE FREE TO RUN WILLLD!
HAHAHAHA
CHAK
OPEN
CLOSE
VMMMM
TIME TO END IT -- GET THEM OUT OF HERE...
NOW!
ZOOSH
ZOOSH
ZOOSH
19

BUH BOOM BAOUM BOOM
GOTHAM TACTICAL

FREEEEEE!!
BRAKAKAKA KAKAK BTAM CHOOM

THE JOKER-?!
G-GONE... C-CRAZY... Huh HELP ME... CAN'T STAND ANY MORE!

ONE CHANCE -- AND THE THROW MUST BE PERFECT...

...WHILE THE JOKER RUNS FREE!
HAHA HAHA
20

CHOOM
SPAP
FREE...
HEEYAHAHAHAHAHA AIEEEEE ARAWOOOOOO YAAAHAHA
...THEY'RE FREE...
...ALL OF THEM...
...EXCEPT ONE...
FREE...I'M F-FREEEE...heh... ha...ha...ha... heh.
THEIR KEEPER.
IT WAS SAFER ON THE INSIDE, COMMISH ... ALL HOSTAGES SAVED BUT SEVENTEEN MEN DOWN ON THE OUTSIDE ... SIX OF 'EM OURS... NONE OF 'EM INMATES.
THEY'RE ALL LOOSE... RUNNIN' WILD LIKE A PACK O' MAD DOGS.
21

THEN GOD HELP US, BUT MAYBE...
...KROL WAS RIGHT...

"... AND NOW WE HAVE TO FIND...
WHP WHP WHP WHP WHP
WHP WHP
"... WHO DID IT."

IF I DIDN'T WANT HIS BLOOD SO BADLY...

... I WOULD ALMOST PITY HIM.

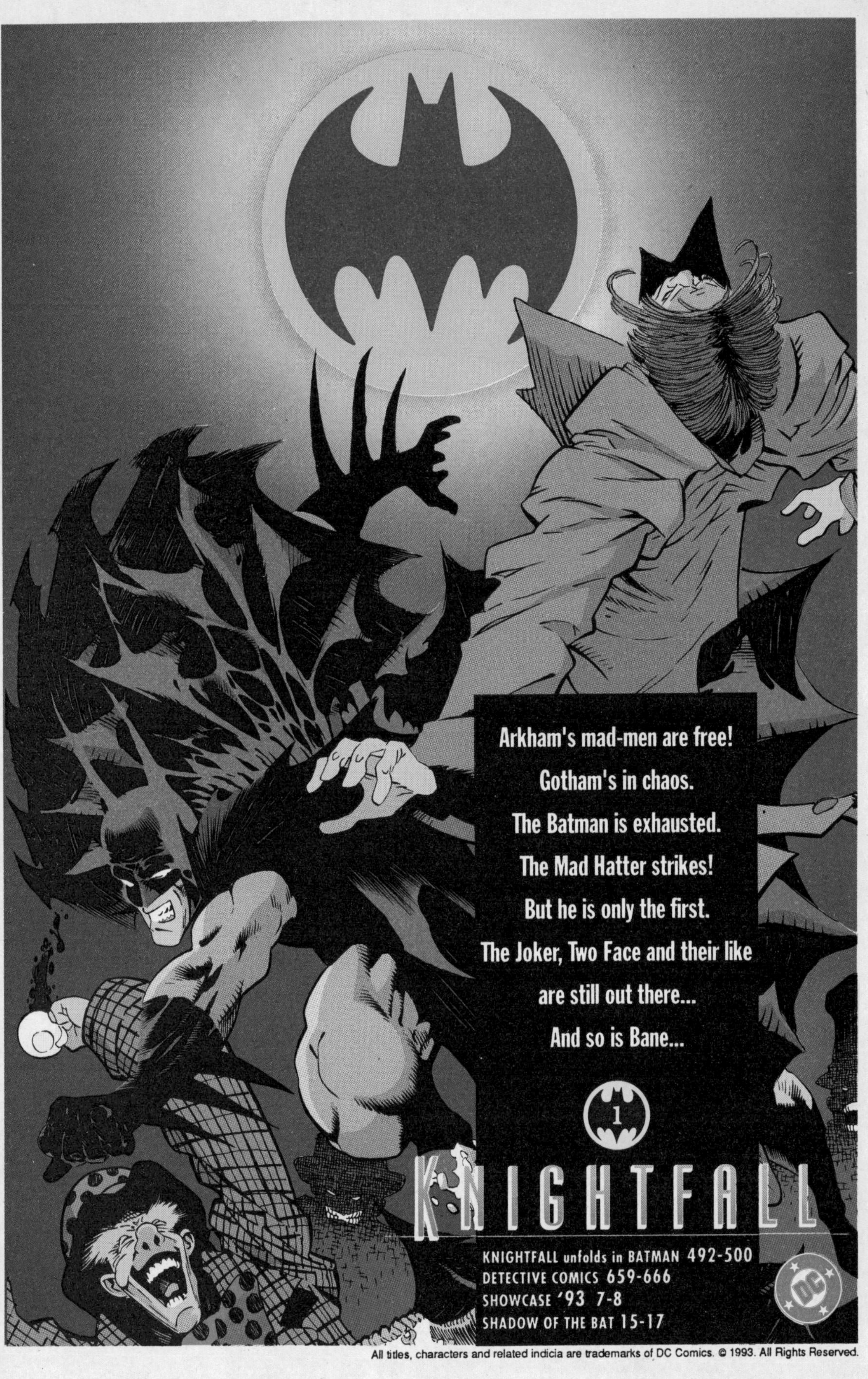
Arkham's mad-men are free!
Gotham's in chaos.
The Batman is exhausted.
The Mad Hatter strikes!
But he is only the first.
The Joker, Two Face and their like
are still out there...
And so is Bane...
1
KNIGHTFALL
KNIGHTFALL unfolds in BATMAN 492-500
DETECTIVE COMICS 659-666
SHOWCASE '93 7-8
SHADOW OF THE BAT 15-17
DC

THEY SEPARATED US, MY DEAR, WHEN THEY LAST SENT ME TO ARKHAM...
GOTHAM ZOO
BUT NOW I'M FREE...
OO-OOH?
CHIMPANZEE
WHZZZZZZZZZZZ
CHANK
BAOUM
...AND SO ARE YOU.
OO-OOO OOH!
1

DOUG MOENCH WRITER · NORM BREYFOGLE ARTIST · ADRIENNE ROY COLORIST · RICHARD STARKINGS LETTERER · SCOTT PETERSON, JORDAN B. GORFINKEL ASST EDITORS · DENNY O'NEIL EDITOR

MY GUESS IS THE BRUTE I TOLD YOU ABOUT -- THE ONE WHO BUSTED UP KILLER CROC...
CALLED HIMSELF BANE -- AND HE'S DEFINITELY GOT IT IN FOR YOU!
YES... THE ONE I CONFRONTED IN THE MANKLIN BROTHERS' HIDEOUT...

COME ON.
IF WE CAN'T FIND THE DEVIL HIMSELF...
... HIS PROGENY ARE LEGION ENOUGH.

THAT'S ONE OF 'EM, ALL RIGHT -- THE MAD HATTER...
BUT WHY IS HE DRIVING AROUND AND AROUND THE SAME BLOCK?
AND WHAT HAPPENED TO HIS STUPID--
"--MONKEY?!"
WELL, IT TOOK A WHILE, MY DEAR...
... BUT SOONER OR LATER, I KNEW THE BIRD WOULD SWOOP LOW ENOUGH FOR YOUR POUNCE.
SKEECH
3

AND SINCE THE BIRD IS A FALCON, MY DEAR -- HARDLY INDIGENOUS TO GOTHAM -- IT MUST BE SOMEONE'S PET...
OO-OOH!
...SOME-ONE WHO IS APPARENTLY WATCHING US...
...AND WHOM WE MAY WISH TO WATCH IN THE FUTURE.
KRMP
BAR
KEV'S
OPTIMIST TIMES
LIFE IS A WONDERLAND
50 DIE IN ECOLOGY DISASTER
GOTHAM NEWS
THE DEVICE IS ATTACHED, MY DEAR -- LET THE FLAPPING THING AWAY...
AND OFF WE GO -- TO PREPARE THE PARTY.
OO-OO-OOH!
HE'S NOT COMIN' AROUND AGAIN -- MUST'VE FOUND HIS CHIMP AND DRIVEN ON UP THE SIDE STREET...
WHICH MEANS I'VE LOST HIM.
COME ON, TALON -- NOT MUCH TO REPORT TO BANE...
"...BUT AT LEAST ONE OF OUR LOONEY STOOGES IS ACTIVE...
HABERDASHERIA
ERIA
SKREETCH
"...AND HOPE-FULLY OUT TO GIVE THE BATMAN FITS."
BRAKAKA
CHUSHH
VEEP
VEEP
VEEP
4

VEEP
VEEP
VEEP
VEEP
YOU GRAB THE HATS, MY DEAR...
OO-OO AHN!
I'LL LEAVE THE INVITATION!
=SKSS= REPORT OF AN ALARM =SKSS= --POSSIBLE BREAK-IN AT HABERDASHERIA ON SALEM =SKSS=
OKAY, I'LL BITE-- WHAT'S A "HABER-DASHER-WHO-EE-UH?"
FANCY NAME FOR A PLACE WHERE THEY SELL HATS.
UH OH.
YES... AND LET'S BEAT THE POLICE TO THE SCENE.
TURBO
TEK
BROOOMMM
OIL TANKER GROUNDED
ELECTRIC CARS: CLEAN/ POOR RANGE
5

NINE RANDOM FREAKOUTS ALREADY, RESULTIN' IN SIX DEATHS WITH NO RHYME OR REASON -- NO CONNECTIONS, NO MOTIVES...
AN' EXHUMATION'S NOTHIN', MONTOYA, COMPARED TO THIS STINK.
JOKER
RIDDLER
TWO-FACE
POISON IVY
KILLER CROC
AMYGDALA
MAXIE ZEUS
CORNELIUS STIRK
SCARECROW
ZSASZ
FILM FREAK
MAD HATTER
IT'S BAD, ALL RIGHT, BUT GIVEN THIS LIST, BULLOCK... MAYBE WE'RE LUCKY THERE'VE ONLY BEEN NINE INCIDENTS SO FAR.
YOU'RE FORGETTIN' IT ONLY GETS WORSE FROM HERE!
BIG DADDY DOUGHNUTS
BIG DADDY DOUGHNUTS

VEEP VEEP VEEP VEEP
ERIA
THE MAD HATTER, ALL RIGHT -- THE FIRST OF THE MAJOR ONES TO MAKE A MOVE...

VEEP VEEP VEEP VEEP
Hold onto Your Hats!
JERVIS TETCH
Requests the Pleasure of
Your Company at
A TEA PARTY!
Date: TONIGHT
Time: ASAP
Place: TENNIEL ESTA
THAT'S SOME KIND OF INVITATION CARD?!
YES-- TO TEA.
... AND HE WANTS US TO BE GUESTS OF HONOR AT HIS LATEST CELEBRATION OF MADNESS.

VEEP VEEP VEEP VEEP
EEOOEEOO
AND IT'S NOT POLITE TO BE LATE.

VEEP VEEP VEEP VEEP
RIA

VEEP VEEP VEEP VEEP
EEOOEE
RIA
SKREECH
POLICE
7

HERE WE GO, MY DEAR -- THE LAST HAT IS DONE...
ARRANGE THEM IN THEIR PLACES, WILL YOU?
OO-OO-WAHH!
--NINE SEPARATE CASES OF VIOLENT CRIME ALREADY, DR. FLANDERS, ALL APPARENTLY LINKED TO THE MASS BREAK-OUT AT ARKHAM ASYLUM. IS THIS WHAT WE CAN EXPECT?
THE ONLY THING WE CAN EXPECT, PETER, IS THE UNEXPECTED...
RIGHT NOW, YOU SEE, THESE MENTALLY DIVERGENT PATIENTS ARE EXTREMELY DISORIENTED AND ALIENATED...
THEREFORE, THEY HAVE NO REAL MOTIVES IN THE TRADITIONAL SENSE, NOR CAN THEIR ACTIONS BE ANTICIPATED.
NO MOTIVE, DR. FLANDERS? NOT EVEN REVENGE?
WELL, WITHOUT GETTING OVERLY HYSTERICAL, PETER, SOME OF THEM MAY INDEED HARBOR GRUDGES OVER REAL OR IMAGINED SLIGHTS...
"SLIGHTS?"
8

YOU MUST UNDERSTAND, PETER, THAT THESE PATIENTS ARE CONFUSED -- AND MAY RESENT PAST TREATMENT AT THE HANDS OF WARDENS, ORDERLIES, THE POLICE, PROSECUTORS, JUDGES, EVEN A PARENT...
ONE MIGHT ADD THE ONLY COMMON LINK SHARED BY MOST, IF NOT ALL, OF THOSE FORMERLY INCARCERATED AT ARKHAM -- THE BATMAN...
INDEED, PETER, THE BATMAN'S EXCESSIVE FORCE MAY WELL COME BACK TO HAUNT --
...AND IF I WERE HIM --

-- I WOULD VIEW THIS MASS ESCAPE AS MY WORST NIGHTMARE COME TRUE...

"... AND, RIGHT NOW, I WOULD FIND IT VERY DIFFICULT TO SLEEP."
"FINALLY, PETER, WE AGREE."
ONLY FIVE MORE MILES TO TENNIEL ESTATES -- WANT ME TO CALL GORDON?

NO -- NO POLICE.
THERE MAY BE ENOUGH BULLETS FLYING AS IT IS -- AND I DON'T WANT ANY STUNTS FROM YOU EITHER.
HEY, I'M COOL -- JUST TELL ME WHAT YOU WANT.
9

THERE MAY BE OTHER "GUESTS" AT THIS "TEA PARTY" -- AND THEY MAY STILL BE HEAVILY ARMED.
YOU'RE STRICTLY BACKUP.
-BUT--
RESENT ME ALL YOU WANT-- BUT DON'T FORGET IT.
VRAOWW
WELCOME, WELCOME, ONE AND ALL! APOLOGIES FOR MAKING YOU LEAVE YOUR WEAPONS AT THE GATE, BUT THEY WILL BE RETURNED SHOULD THE POLICE ARRIVE BEFORE OUR GUEST OF HONOR.
RIGHT NOW, IF YOU WOULD BE GOOD ENOUGH TO DON THE PARTY HATS AT YOUR PLACE SETTINGS... OUR FESTIVITIES MAY COMMENCE!
THIS IS STUPID, HATTER, I DON'T WEAR A HAT FOR NOBODY.
YEAH -- WHEN YOU INVITED US TO YOUR PARTY AFTER THE BREAKOUT, YOU SAID WE COULD KILL THE BATMAN.
SO, WHERE IS HE? AND WHAT'S WEARIN' HATS GOT TO DO WITH--
PUT ON THE HATS!
NOW!
10

THAAAT'S BETTER... Eh, MY DEAR?
CLAP CLAP CLAP
OO-OO-AHH!
AND SINCE MY COMPUTERIZED HAT-TRANSMISSIONS ARE NOW VOICE-ACTIVATED, IT REMAINS ONLY TO SAY...
HATS-- INDUCE TRANCE.
PING PING PING PING
THE HATBAND CIRCUITRY WORKS PERFECTLY, MY DEAR -- SURROUNDING THEIR SKULLS WITH SIGNALS THAT ALTER THEIR ALPHA BRAINWAVES...
...MAKING THEM BIOLOGICAL ROBOTS-- ZOMBIES OBEDIENT TO THE WHIMS OF MY VOICE, TRANSMITTED THROUGH MY HAT TO THEIRS.
TOO BAD THE JOKER, TWO-FACE, SCARECROW AND THE OTHERS FAILED TO ACCEPT MY INVITATION... BUT THEN, THEIR ILK MIGHT HAVE TRIED TO SPOIL THE PARTY...
IN ANY CASE, FILM FREAK, I'M GLAD YOU ACCEPTED THE INVITATION, BECAUSE I'M GOING TO DELEGATE OUR FIRST ITEM OF BUSINESS TO YOU...
11

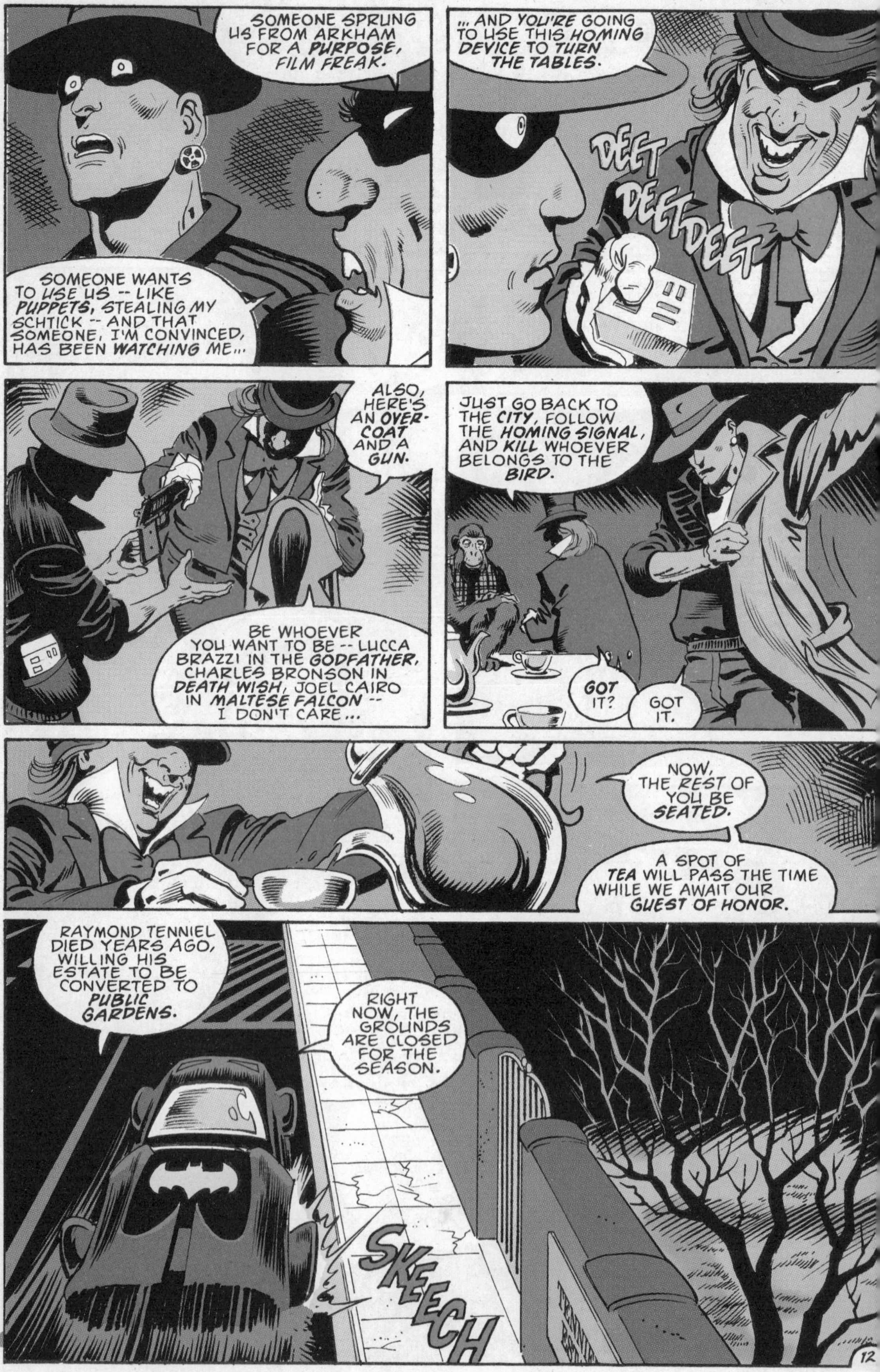

NOW, THE REST OF YOU BE SEATED.

A SPOT OF TEA WILL PASS THE TIME WHILE WE AWAIT OUR GUEST OF HONOR.

RAYMOND TENNIEL DIED YEARS AGO, WILLING HIS ESTATE TO BE CONVERTED TO PUBLIC GARDENS.

RIGHT NOW, THE GROUNDS ARE CLOSED FOR THE SEASON.

SKEECH

12

AND MAD HATTER'S USING THE PLACE BECAUSE--
BECAUSE SIR JOHN TENNIEL ILLUSTRATED LEWIS CARROLL'S WONDERLAND STORIES... AND BECAUSE MADNESS KNOWS NO SEASON OR--

Ahn...
HEY-- YOU ALL RIGHT? MAYBE WE SHOULDN'T--

I'M FINE.

WE GOT BIG TROUBLE, BANE-- SOME KIND OF HOMING DEVICE.
IT WAS ON TALON'S LEG, BUT HOW IT COULD'VE--
GIVE IT TO ME.

KRNCH

SOMEONE DOWN IN THE STREET -- CASING THE HOTEL-- SOME KIND OF ELECTRONIC DEVICE IN HIS HAND...
LEMME SEE.
13

NINTH
NORTHPOINT
HOMING SIGNAL JUST CUT OUT, HATTER... AT NORTHPOINT AND NINTH...
HOTEL

THERE'S A HOTEL HERE. I'M GOING TO TRY THE SERVICE ENTRANCE IN THE ALLEY...
YOU DO THAT, FREAKIE-BOY.
ANYONE FOR MORE TEA?
OO-OO-AHN!

NOW.

CHUSH
REEEEEE!

IT'S ONE OF THE ARKHAM INMATES, ALL RIGHT -- THE ONE CALLED FILM FREAK...
...HEADIN' FOR THE ALLEY.

DON'T MAKE A MOVE, HATTER.
AHAH! OUR GUEST OF HONOR -- AT LAST!
14

YOU STAY HERE...
TEK
FWSH
FWSH
...WHILE I KILL HIM.
SIT DOWN, BATMAN! HAVE A CUP OF TEA...
WHAT'S YOUR GAME THIS TIME, HATTER? WHO IS THIS BANE?
WHAT'S HE AFTER -- AND WHY ARE YOU HELPING HIM?

SERVICE ENTRANCE
IT'S LOCKED, HATTER...

I MAY HAVE TO JUST WATCH THE FRONT ENTRANCE.
TRANS-MITTER AND RECEIVER IN YOUR HAT -- BUT WHO'S USING IT?
Oh, JUST FILM FREAK -- REPORTING ON GOTHAM'S NIGHT LIFE.

ALSO PART OF BANE'S PLAN?
THAT'S THE SECOND TIME YOU'VE MENTIONED THAT NAME... BUT, IN REPLY, I CAN ONLY SAY...
15

...WHO'S BANE?

I'M ...

ENTRANCE

BANE...

SWUKK

...AND YOUR KILLER--

--IS DEAD.

HIS VOICE... THE SAME... THEN IT IS HIM...

HATS-- STIMULATE ADRENAL CORTEX!

YOU WANTED TO KILL THE BATMAN...
...AND HERE'S YOUR CHANCE.
PARTY HEARTY!
TUDT
SHREEEE

SO HOW LONG DOES A "BACKUP" HOLD BACK?!
SWAK
CHUSH
BRAM BRAM BRAM
RAHR!
POK
STOK
POK

BLANG

GUH-H!
WUMP
17

KAFT
CHUT
THE HATTER-- GOING FOR THAT MACHINE-GUN...
...WHICH MEANS I'VE HELD BACK LONG ENOUGH!
SNK SNK
YEEAGHHH!
KRAKT
HATTER!!
SHUMP
BRAK
18

SHREEEE!
WHAT THE --?!
THANK YOU, MY DEAR!

THE *PERFECT* RESPITE IN WHICH TO FINALLY *FINISH OFF* THE --

BRAKAKAK

KRAK

REEEEE

OOF!

!! BAG OF FLEAS!!

DEAD

19

CHOOF
THEY'RE CONTROLLED BY THE *HATS!*
GOTCHA.

KUP
TUP
FRAK
TAK

KUNKT

KRNCH
SKPP
TUMP
KUMP
AIEEEE
EEEEE
KRAKT
21

TRASH
YOU'RE GARBAGE...

...AND YOU'RE DEAD... JUST LIKE THE BATMAN.
HE'S WRONG-- WE'LL GET HIM... I KNOW WE WILL...

HEY, YOU'RE NOT TICKED, ARE YOU? IT WAS ONLY ONE GUN... BUT POINTED AT YOUR BACK.
I SAW IT.

TWO DOWN... MAD HATTER AND THE FILM FREAK...
YEAH -- AND ONLY THE REST OF THE MADHOUSE TO GO.

PLUS BANE.

OO-OOH-AHN

NEXT > THE VENTRILOQUIST & AMYGDOLA!

PUPPETS
IT BEGAN LAST NIGHT.
BY TWIST OF FATE OR MACHINATION, NONE OF THEM KNOW OR CARE.
THE WALLS OF ARKHAM CAME TUMBLING DOWN AND NOW THEY ARE...
FREE!
FREE TO GATHER MY LEGIONS ONCE MORE.
CHUCK DIXON-WRITER NORM BREYFOGLE-GUEST ARTIST ADRIENNE ROY-COLORIST
TIM HARKINS-LETTERER SCOTT PETERSON and DENNIS O'NEIL-EDITORS Batman created by BOB KANE

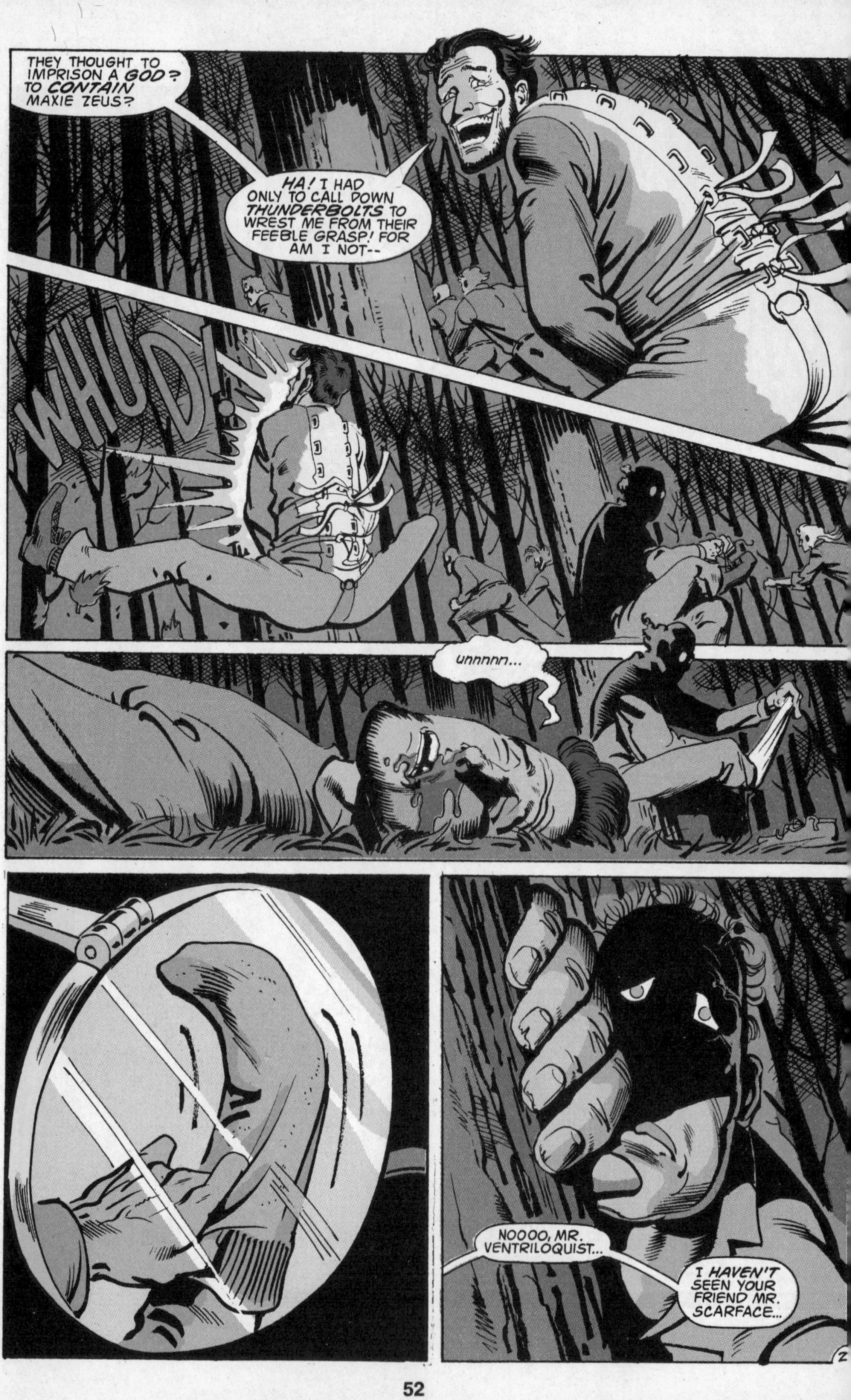

THEY THOUGHT TO IMPRISON A *GOD*? TO *CONTAIN* MAXIE ZEUS?

HA! I HAD ONLY TO CALL DOWN *THUNDERBOLTS* TO WREST ME FROM THEIR FEEBLE GRASP! FOR AM I NOT--

WHUD!

unnnnn...

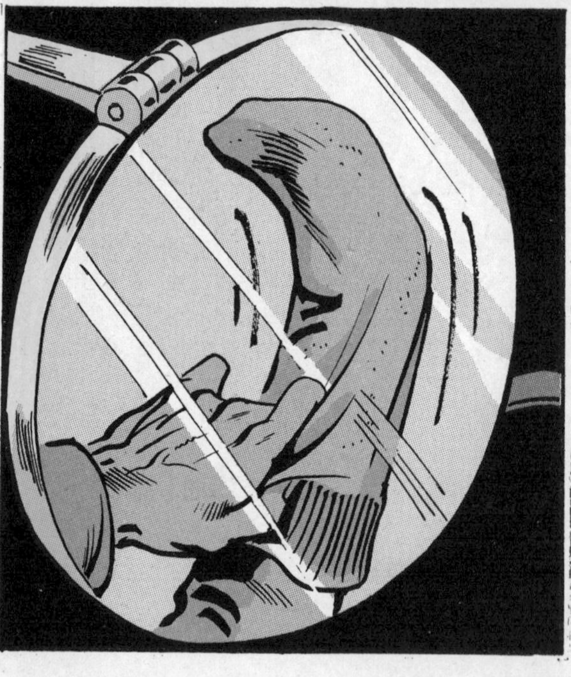

NOOOO, MR. VENTRILOQUIST...
I *HAVEN'T* SEEN YOUR FRIEND MR. SCARFACE...

I REALLY *MUST* FIND HIM. AND I CAN'T DO IT ALONE. COULD *YOU* HELP ME?
I CAN *TRY*, MR. VENTRILOQUIST...

COULD I HELP TOO?
oh.

I CAN HELP YOU FIND YOUR FRIEND. I'M KINDA LOST TOO. SOMEBODY BLEW UP MY ROOM.
THEY CALL YOU AMYGDALA, DO THEY NOT?
30086
YOU'RE A VERRRRY *GIG GOY*.
50725

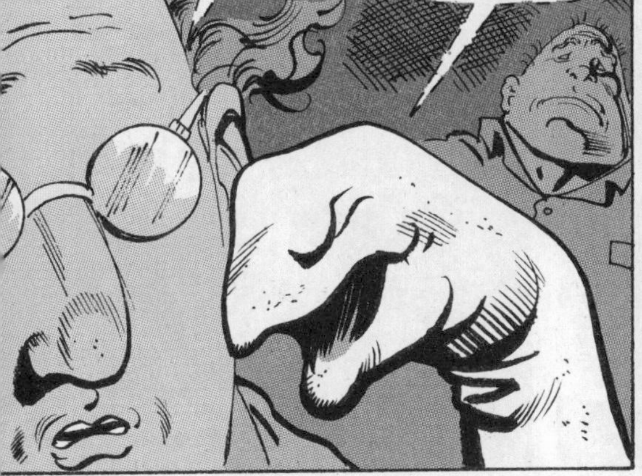
AMYGDALA IS VERY DANGEROUS. THE DOCTORS AT ARKHAM EXPERIMENTED ON HIS BRAIN. HE'S QUITE UNCONTROLLABLE.
THEN WE MUST GE CAUTIOUS IF WE'RE TO USE HIM.

YOU MAY HELP ME FIND *SCARFACE*, AMYGDALA. I AM THE VENTRILOQUIST.
AND WHAT'S YOUR LITTLE *FRIEND'S* NAME?
uh... SOCKO.
AM I SUPPOSED TO GET MY MEDICINE SOON?
3

THAT WAS LAST NIGHT.

THIS IS NOW.

I HALF EXPECTED THIS. OBVIOUSLY, IT'S BANE'S WORK.

BUT WHY?

NO SIGN OF ENTRY WOUNDS. NO EVIDENCE THAT A WEAPON WAS USED.
IT LOOKS LIKE EVERY BONE IN HIS BODY IS BROKEN. AS HARD AS IT IS TO BELIEVE, FILM FREAK WAS BEATEN TO DEATH BY SOME-ONE USING ONLY THEIR BARE FISTS.

ARE YOU ALL RIGHT, ROBIN?
uh... SURE, BATMAN.

WE'D BETTER KEEP ROLLING. I WANT TO STAY AHEAD OF THE POLICE ON THIS.

HE'S DEAD?
THEY DON'T GET ANY DEADER THAN THIS.
YOU GUYS WANT TO STEP LIGHTER? THIS IS A CRIME SCENE.

LIEUTENANT KITCH, I DIDN'T KNOW YOU WERE CATCHING.
I'M NOT. I WAS TWO BLOCKS AWAY WHEN THE CALL CAME IN. I'LL STICK UNTIL HOMICIDE GETS HERE.
WANT I SHOULD RADIO FOR A MEAT WAGON?

IT'S CALLED A MEDICAL EXAMINER'S VAN, PATROLMAN. EVEN A SKEL LIKE THIS DESERVES SOME RESPECT.
YOU KNOW THIS ONE, EL TEE?

ONE OF THE ARKHAM INMATES. WENT BY THE NAME FILM FREAK. A LONG NIGHT JUST GOT LONGER.
BETTER PUT A CALL IN TO THE COMMISSIONER.
TELL HIM WE DON'T HAVE TO LOOK FOR THIS ONE ANYMORE.
5

BACK TO GOTHAM INSIDER. OUR JEST IS DR. SIMPSON FLANDERS, NICAL PSYCHOLOGIST AND SOCIATE AT ARKHAM ASYLUM--
GOTHA INSIDER
-- WHICH IS MUCH IN THE NEWS TONIGHT. WHAT CAN WE EXPECT FROM THE MASS ESCAPE FROM ARKHAM, DOCTOR?
EXCUSE ME FOR SAYING SO, LINDA, BUT I THINK THE MEDIA ARE ACTING A BIT... HYSTERICAL.
AS I'VE DETAILED IN MY CURRENT BOOK, "I'M SANE AND SO ARE YOU," THESE PATIENTS ARE MERELY MISUNDERSTOOD.
THEY ARE CRYING OUT FOR HELP, LINDA.
I'm Sane and s YOU!
THERE HAVE BEEN A DOZEN *HOMICIDES* SINCE THE BREAKOUT.
WE'RE TALKING ABOUT THE MOST DANGEROUS COLLECTION OF PSYCHOPATHS EVER ASSEMBLED. THEY ARE *HARDLY* "MISUNDERSTOOD."
THAT'S YOUR INNATE PREJUDICE TOWARD THE MENTALLY DIVERGENT--
"MENTALLY DIVERGENT"? *THAT'S* A NEW ONE.
IT'S IN MY BOOK.
AND LET ME MAKE ANOTHER POINT. THESE PATIENTS ARE CONFUSED, LOST. THEY CANNOT OPERATE IN THE OUTSIDE WORLD.
YOU THINK ARE A DAN SOCIET

"WELL, THEY'RE IN GREATER DANGER FROM US THAN WE ARE FROM THEM."
WE'LL STAY MOBILE FOR NOW. CHANCES ARE WE CAN NAIL MORE OF THE ESCAPEES BEFORE THEY CAN GET TO DEEP COVER.
NOT THAT I'M COMFORTABLE WITH THAT STRATEGY.
I'M SURE WE WON'T HAVE TO LOOK FOR ALL OF THEM.
SOME OF THEM WILL BE LOOKING FOR US.
SKIDS
LOVE
JUST DO IT
F.O.I.A. THE OXYMORON
MAYBE SOME OF THEM ALREADY ARE.
NO JUSTICE, NO PEACE
DREAM BIG!
HEAVY HEAVY CLUB
SOLID BLOOD
POST NO BILLS
DEMONZ
BEEP
WSHSHSH
BEEP
I'D PREFER TO BE ACTING MORE AND RE-ACTING LESS. BUT THERE'S NO RHYME OR REASON TO ANY OF THIS.
YET.
THAT'S WHY WE HAVE TO MOVE FAST. THE REALLY DANGEROUS ONES WILL BE THOSE WHO GET A CHANCE TO PLAN.
7

"THEN THE RANDOM VIOLENCE TURNS TO MORE DELIBERATE MAYHEM."
THE TAP ROOM
ah-hem.
GENTLEMEN...
YO. LOOK WHO IT IS.

WE'RE LOOKING FOR SCARFACE. HAVE ANY OF YOU GENTLEMEN SEEN HIM?
PERHAPS I MIGHT EVEN ENLIST YOUR AID IN SEARCHING FOR HIM.

HA HA HA HEE HEE HOO HOO HA HA

LAUGH AT SOCKO, WILL YOU?
WELL, CHUCKLE ALL YOU WANT AT ME...
8

YOU'RE LAUGHING AT MY LITTLE FRIEND?
NOBODY LAUGHS AT MY LITTLE FRIEND!
...GUT I THINK YOU'D GEST TAKE MY PAL AMYGDALA MORE SERIOUSLY.
CHSH
POM
WHAT'S SO FUNNY?
SLURP
SOCKO, PERHAPS YOU'RE NOT UP TO THE DEMANDS I'M PLACING ON YOU. AND AMYGDALA IS TOO... ENERGETIC.
I NEED SOMEONE WITH FINESSE TO HELP ME FIND SCARFACE.
9

OOOPS.
DID I LOSE MY TEMPER AGAIN? IS MR. SOCKO *MAD* AT ME?
THOSE GENTLEMEN WEREN'T BEING VERY HELPFUL ANYWAY.

I NEED YOU TO HELP ME GET SOMETHING.
AND THEN WE'LL FIND MR. SCARFACE?
PRECISELY.
AND *THEN* I'LL GET MY MEDICINE?
WE'LL SEE.

METAPHYSIQUE IS COMING!
WORLD NEWS
OPERATION CENSORED WAR
BOMBING FOOTAGE SPIKED
THERE HAS TO BE A METHOD TO ALL THIS MADNESS, ROBIN.
YOU DON'T THINK THESE MADMEN ARE *CO-OPERATING* WITH ONE ANOTHER?

10

NO. THEIR DEMENTIAS MAKE THEM ALL TOO EGOCENTRIC TO COLLABORATE.
BUT THEY WERE FREED AND ARMED BY SOMEONE ON THE OUTSIDE.
SHOTS FIRED GATE AND MYERS...
MAYBE THIS IS ALL PART OF A MASTER PLAN.
WHO COULD PROFIT BY ALL THIS CHAOS?
WHAT'S YOUR TWENTY, BRAVO NINE?
WHAT ABOUT BANE-THE ONE WHO TOOK OUT CROC? THE GUY WHO WAS GOING TO CLEAN JEAN PAUL'S CLOCK UNTIL HE REALIZED IT WASN'T YOU?
HE'D BE MY FIRST CHOICE. WHOEVER HE IS HE HAS IT IN FOR ME PERSONALLY.
PROWLER CALL. ONE NINETEEN PALMER.
THIS COULDN'T HAVE HAPPENED AT A WORSE TIME.
MEANING?
YOU'RE NOT REALLY AT THE TOP OF YOUR FORM, BATMAN. YOU'VE BEEN SICK...
STOLEN CAR, BACK LOT AT BEIDERMAN'S.
AND YOU THINK I CAN SIT THIS ONE OUT?
CHECK ON SILENT ALARM AT JOYBOY TOYS.
NO. IT'S JUST...
A TOY STORE BREAK-IN. THAT'S THE KIND OF CALL WE'RE LOOKING FOR.
...NEVILLE AVENUE AND FRONT.
11

"THE MORE OFFBEAT THE POLICE CALL, THE MORE LIKELY WE'LL FIND AN ESCAPEE."

JOY-BOY TOYS

KEV'S

OH, THIS WON'T DO. THIS WON'T DO AT *ALL*.

THERE ISN'T THE *SELECTION* I HAD ANTICIPATED.

NONE OF THESE TURN YOU ON, *HUH?*

NOT QUITE. I CAN'T VERY WELL ENLIST THE AID OF A DUCK TO RESCUE SCARFACE.

MAYBE IT'S TIME YOU *FORGOT* AGOUT THIS SCARFACE GUY. HE NEVER DID ANYTHING TO TRY AND GET YOU OUT OF ARKHAM, RIGHT?
MAYGE IT'S TIME YOU FOUND A *NEW* PARTNER.

HOW CAN YOU *SAY* THAT? I'M *NOTHING* WITHOUT SCARFACE.
THEY'RE GEST GUDDIES! WAAUUGH!

DID YOU HEAR THAT?
SOUNDS LIKE A CAR PULLING UP.
uh-oh.
12

LET ME HANDLE THIS UNTIL WE KNOW WHAT WE'RE UP AGAINST.
BUT YOU'RE GOING TO NEED HELP.
DO AS I SAY, ROBIN.

I MIGHT NEED YOU OUT HERE. I'LL BE ALL RIGHT IN THERE.

SURE.
YOU CAN BARELY STAND UP NOW.

TWO FALCONS IN ONE NIGHT?
I DON'T THINK SO.
13

IT'S ONLY YOU.

OH MY GOSH! BATMAN!

ENORMOUS NORM

DOPEY DIXON

WARNER WOLF

SING-SONG SALLY

SING-SONG GALLY

TIME FOR YOU TO COME WITH ME, VENTRILOQUIST.

I'LL GO ALONG QUIETLY, BATMAN. NO TROUBLE FROM ME. NO SIR.

JEEPERS! LOOK OUT BEHIND YOU! A MONSTER!

SHUT UP, YOU RAT!

MIKEY MOUSE

14

I'M NOT IN THE MOOD FOR OLD JOKES, VENTRILOQUIST.
KEEP YOUR HANDS WHERE I CAN SEE THEM.
LEAVE MY FRIENDS ALONE!
DON'T TOUCH THEM!
I'LL HURT YOU! I'LL HURT YOU REAL BAD!
15

JOY-BOY TOYS

LED ME RIGHT TO HIM, TALON. GOOD BOY.

JUST HAVE TO FIND A PLACE TO WATCH THE ACTION.

THE BIRD'S A NICE TOUCH. BUT YOU SHOULD PICK ONE NATIVE TO GOTHAM.

SURE. MAYBE SOME *SISSY* BIRD. LIKE A *ROBIN!*

TEAR HIS *FACE* OFF!

16

KRASH!
YOU MAKE ME SO ANGRY!
BIG SQUIRT
BUZZO THE CLOWN
YOU MAKE ME WANT TO HURT YOU!
CRUSH YOUR SKULL! BREAK YOUR BONES!
KRATCH
BRANDY
BRANDY DOLLS SOLD HERE!
BRANDY
UNNNH!
SWUMP
HI! I'M BRANDY!
BRANDY
17

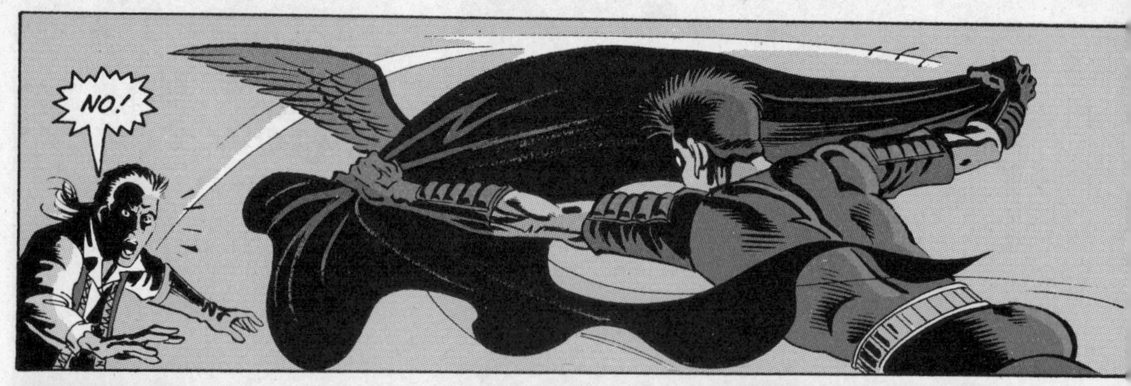
NO!

MAYBE YOU WANT TO TELL ME WHY YOU'VE BEEN FOLLOWING US.

YOU LITTLE *CREEP!*
STUP
IF YOU'VE HARMED ONE FEATHER ON TALON'S HEAD...

QUAK
THE BUZZARD'S *FINE*, BUDDY. BUT YOU'RE GOING TO NEED AN *ICEPACK* IN THE MORNING.

18

WISEGUY, HUH?
I HATE WISEGUYS.
UNF!
SWAK
SPOK
KILL YOU!
19

HURT YOU! BREAK YOU! KILL YOU!
YOU MAKE ME SO MAD!
ARRRR!
HEAD ON FIRE! HURTS! HURTS!
WANT MY MEDICINE... TAKE PAIN AWAY... CAN I HAVE MY MEDICINE... NOW?
I HAVE JUST WHAT YOU NEED, AMYGDALA.
THE SAME DOSE I GAVE YOU LAST TIME WE MET.
SHOKK
UnNnH!
20

KIKKK
YOU PUT UP A GOOD FRONT, KID...

SNK
BUT YOU'LL NEVER GET A CHANCE TO WALK THE WALK.
BIRD. ANSWER ME, BIRD.

WHAT IS IT? I'M KINDA BUSY. I GOT THIS ROBIN BRAT DOWN FOR THE COUNT.
LEAVE HIM. I DO NOT WANT TO SHOW OUR HAND THIS SOON.
aw...
OBEY ME, BIRD. COME TO ME. TROGG CAN TAKE OVER THE SURVEILLANCE.
YOUR LUCKY NIGHT. YOU GET A STAY OF EXECUTION, KID.

SEE YOU LATER, PUNK.

NOT IF I SEE YOU FIRST.
21

FREDDY
FLY
BUZZO
THE
CLOWN

NOW. GET HIM WHILE HE'S WEAK.
NO. HE'S STILL DANGEROUS. HELP ME FIND SCARFACE.

I SAY WE KILL HIM.
SCARFACE WILL KNOW WHAT TO DO.

ALL UNITS-- BATES SCHOOL FOR GIRLS-- TEN THIRTY IN PROGRESS--
ROBIN?
WEnt Bird-Watching -R
SUSPECT IS CALLING HIMSELF ZSASZ-- HE HAS HOSTAGES-- REQUESTING TACTICAL UNITS---

The Batman dares not rest.
The crazed slasher Zsasz will
butcher a school
full of innocent girls!
Batman's body will stand
further punishment.
But can his mind?
And Bane is still out there...
KNIGHTFALL
3
BATMAN 493
by Moench and Breyfogle
KNIGHTFALL unfolds in
BATMAN 492-500
DETECTIVE COMICS 659-666
SHOWCASE '93 7-8
SHADOW OF THE BAT
15-17
DC

RACING FOR MY GRAVE, ALREADY DEAD.
BUT I CAN'T REST, NOT AFTER THE ARKHAM BREAKOUT-- THIRTY-ODD MURDERS ALREADY, AND ALL THE WORK OF MINOR MADMEN.
OF THE FOUR MAJOR ONES TO MAKE A MOVE, THE MAD HATTER AND AMYGDALA HAVE BEEN CAPTURED, THE VENTRILOQUIST IS STILL AT LARGE, AND THE FILM FREAK HIMSELF HAS BEEN MURDERED.
IT'S BARELY BEGUN, BUT THE GRAVE IS RUSHING CLOSER, AND NOW...
SKSS ZSASZ, SERIAL KILLER RECENTLY ESCAPED FROM ARKHAM SKSS HOLED UP IN THE BATES SCHOOL FOR WOMEN SKSS HOSTAGES SKSS SEND TACTICAL SQUADS AT ONCE SKSS
NO REST, NOT FOR THE WICKED... NOR THOSE WHO DARE DEAL WITH THEM.

RED SLASH

DOUG MOENCH - WRITER / NORM BREYFOGLE - ARTIST / ADRIENNE ROY - COLORIST / TIM HARKINS - LETTERER
JORDAN B. GORFINKEL - ASS'T. EDITOR / DENNIS O'NEIL - EDITOR / BATMAN CREATED BY BOB KANE

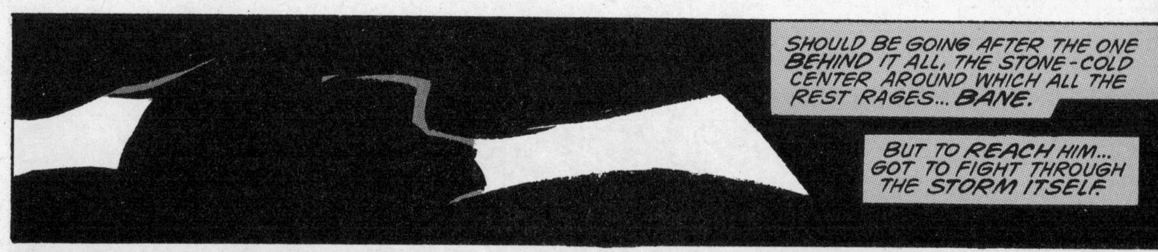

SHOULD BE GOING AFTER THE ONE BEHIND IT ALL, THE STONE-COLD CENTER AROUND WHICH ALL THE REST RAGES... BANE.
BUT TO REACH HIM... GOT TO FIGHT THROUGH THE STORM ITSELF.

CHAOS--PERFECTLY ORCHESTRATED WITH A SINGLE MASTER STROKE.

FREE THE MADMEN... FREE THE MONSTERS...

...AND LET THEM RUN WILD.

YOU SEE THE MARKS?

SELF-INFLICTED, EVERY ONE... ALL LOVINGLY ETCHED...

SOUVENIRS... TO TAKE EVERYWHERE.

CRIMINAL PSYCHOLOGY

ABNORMAL BREYFOGLE

DENNY'S DEMENTIA

MADNESS OF MOENCH

HYSTERICAL HARKINS

RANDOM KILLINGS OF ROY

GRUESOME GORFINKEL

AND WHILE I'M CHASING THE THUNDER, PUTTING OUT ALL THE FIRES, BURNING MYSELF OUT, BANE IS RESTING, ENJOYING THE SPECTACLE...

...WAITING FRESH AT THE CENTER... WAITING TO CUT ME OFF AT MY GRAVE.

A MAP OF HARDENED BLOOD CHARTING MY EVERY SIN, ALL MY GLORY... ONE LITTLE SLASH FOR EVERY BIG ONE...
...EACH SCAR A KILL... EACH SCORE... A SCORE OF LIVES.
2

LOOK AT YOU, TOO TERRIFIED TO SO MUCH AS WHIMPER... BUT DEEP INSIDE, WHERE ALL THE RED IS SO BARELY BOUND, I KNOW YOU'RE ASKING...
"HOW MANY OF US... WILL BECOME PART OF HIM?"

MAYBE ALL OF YOU, MAYBE ONLY SOME...
...BUT SURELY AT LEAST, SAY... THREE OF YOU.

ONE THING IS CERTAIN...
I INTEND TO SAVOR THIS NIGHT IN PEACE, AND THE SUREST WAY TO GET UNDER AND INTO MY SKIN... IS BY MAKING A FUSS.

KLATCH
KLITCH

LOCKED US IN... GONNA DIE...
A FUSS--? WE SHOULD HAVE JUMPED HIM--RIPPED HIS EYES OUT.
EASY TO SAY NOW... NOW THAT HE'S GONE.

SOMEBODY GO AROUND FRONT AND FIND KITCH-- TELL HIM THIS LOOKS LIKE THE LAST OF 'EM FOR NOW!
3

LIEUTENANT KITCH-- MOST OF THE WOMEN GOT OUT THE BACK-- BEING TAKEN TO HOSPITALS FOR TRAUMA COUNSELING...
BATES SCHOOL FOR WOMEN
MOST--?

STILL SOME FIFTEEN RESIDENT STUDENTS UNACCOUNTED FOR, SIR-- AND ONE OF THE ESCAPED WOMEN CLAIMS SHE BROKE FREE OF A GROUP ZSASZ WAS HERDING INTO THE LIBRARY.
HER CONDITION?
PRETTY HYSTERICAL BUT CONVINCING-- AND IT MAKES SENSE...

IF THOSE FIFTEEN AREN'T STASHED IN THE LIBRARY-- OR AT LEAST SCATTERED IN DIFFERENT PLACES IN THERE-- THEN THEY'RE PROBABLY DEAD.
WE NEVER ASSUME THAT, OFFICER.

THEN... HE'S STILL GOT FIFTEEN HOSTAGES, SIR.
FIFTEEN OR FIVE-HUNDRED-- THE SITUATION REMAINS THE SAME.
HOW LONG SINCE AXTON WENT IN THERE?
GOING ON TWENTY MINUTES.

TOO LONG.
WANT ME TO TRY TO RAISE HIM, SIR?
I TOLD YOU-- THE NOISE MIGHT GIVE HIM AWAY... AND I STILL CAN'T BELIEVE THE ENTIRE FORCE ISN'T EQUIPPED WITH EARPHONES FOR THOSE THINGS.
I'VE GOT ONE...

GOTHAM TACTICAL
BENSON--TACTICAL SQUAD--AND AFTER WHAT HAPPENED TO MY BUDDIES AT ARKHAM, I'M READY.
HOW'RE YOU GETTING IN?
ONLY ONE MAN IN SO FAR--NAME'S AXTON...
THROUGH THAT WINDOW THERE--INTO ONE OF THE CLASSROOMS.
CAR'S ALMOST OUT OF CONTROL... GRAVE GETTING TOO CLOSE...
HOW MANY SCARS IN ZSASZ'S SKIN? HOW MANY TIMES HAS HE SLASHED HIMSELF IN SICK CELEBRATION?
NOT ONE MORE--NOT ONE.
NO CHOICE--IF THE LIBRARY WINDOWS FACE NOTHING BUT THE CENTRAL COURTYARD, THEN I HAVE TO GO IN THE SAME WAY AS AXTON.
JUST SPEAK SOFTLY, LIEUTENANT KITCH, AND I'LL HEAR EVERYTHING THROUGH THE EARPLUG...
I MAY NOT BE ABLE TO RESPOND... BUT I'LL CLICK THE BUTTON EVERY TWO MINUTES OR SO.
5

HE'LL BE BACK... BACK TO KILL US ALL...
Oh, STOP YOUR SNIVELING, ANN!
IF HE DOES COME BACK, I SAY WE JUMP HIM--ALL AT ONCE! NO WAY HE CAN KILL US ALL.

BUT HE COULD KILL SOME OF US--AND JUMPING HIM MIGHT BE THE THING THAT FORCES HIM TO DO IT.
DIE... WE'RE GONNA DIE...

AXTON--? YOU FIND SOMETHING--?

ALL RIGHT, SO WE HOLD BACK AS LONG AS WE'RE ALL OKAY... BUT THE MOMENT HE TOUCHES ONE OF US--ANY ONE OF US--WE ALL POUNCE ON HIM, KICKING AND CLAWING WHERE IT HURTS MOST.
RIGHT--?

DIE... ALL GONNA DIE...

aw, NO... YOU FOUND BLOOD...

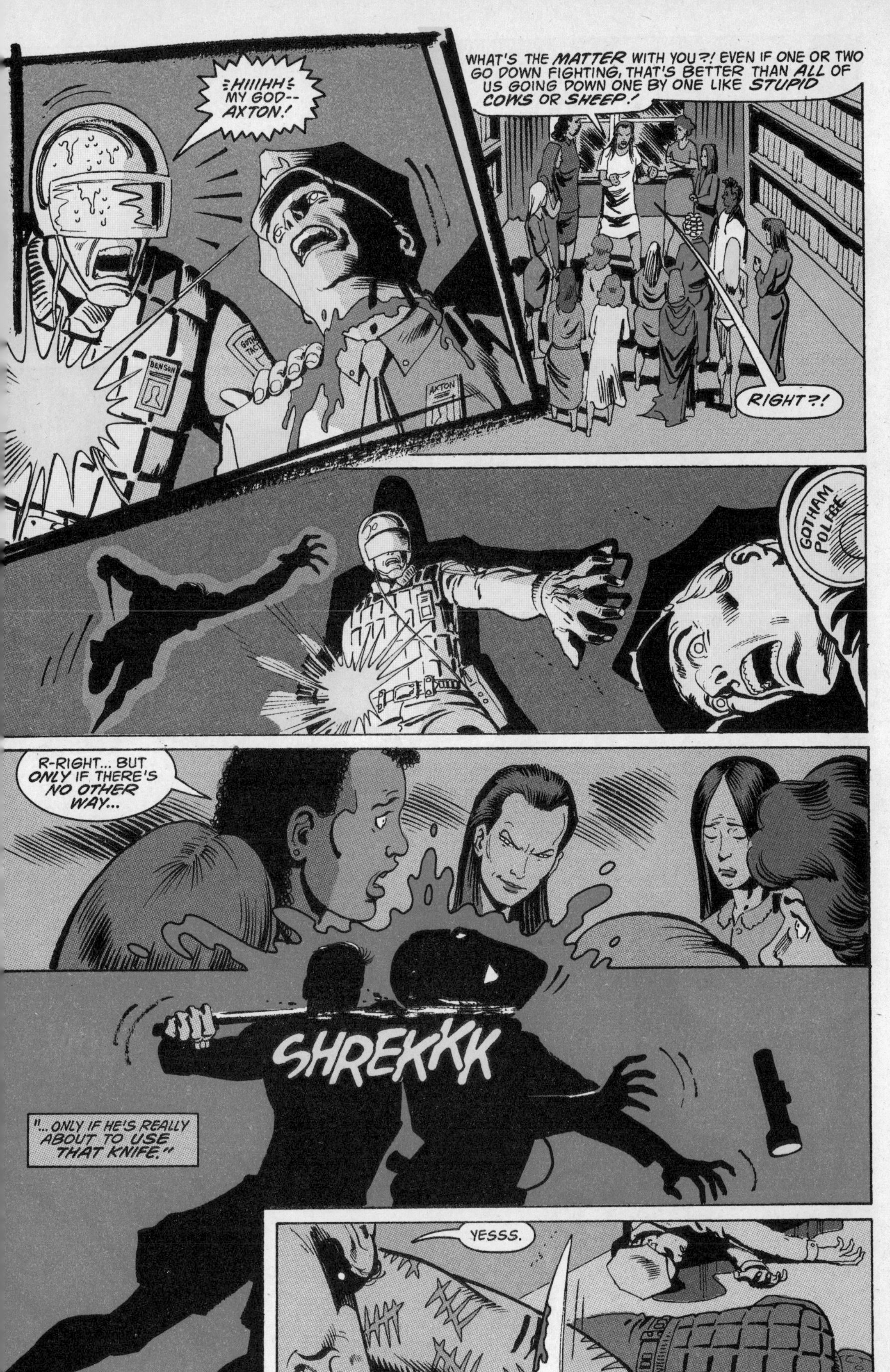
HIIIHH! MY GOD-- AXTON!
WHAT'S THE MATTER WITH YOU?! EVEN IF ONE OR TWO GO DOWN FIGHTING, THAT'S BETTER THAN ALL OF US GOING DOWN ONE BY ONE LIKE STUPID COWS OR SHEEP!
RIGHT?!
GOTHAM POLICE
R-RIGHT... BUT ONLY IF THERE'S NO OTHER WAY...
SHREKKK
"...ONLY IF HE'S REALLY ABOUT TO USE THAT KNIFE."
YESSS.
7

--TENSE STANDOFF CONTINUES AT GOTHAM'S BATES SCHOOL FOR WOMEN, WHERE POLICE ARE UNABLE TO MOVE WITHOUT RISK TO HOSTAGES' LIVES...
LOTTA COPS, BANE-- BUT NO BATMAN YET.
IN OTHER NEWS...
HE'LL BE THERE, BIRD.
BATE'S S
FOR WOM
I THINK MAYBE THE BATMAN'S RIPE FOR HIS FALL RIGHT NOW.
NO. HE'S PHYSICALLY WEAKENED-- AND DEPLETED MORE WITH EACH NEW EXPLOSION OF MADNESS--BUT HIS MIND IS STILL STRONG...
PROBABLY--BUT I'M BEGINNIN' TO WONDER ABOUT HIM, BANE--ESPECIALLY AFTER RUNNIN' INTO HIS LITTLE PARTNER.
THE KID'S GOOD, BUT ANY MAN WHO RELIES ON A KID MAY BE OVERRATED...
HE IS NOT READY TO BE BROKEN... NOT QUITE YET.
KRIK
WHEN HE IS, I WILL KNOW IT... AND THEN, THE PIECES WILL STAY BROKEN.
8

BULLOCK AN' MONTOYA--
MAJOR CRIMES.
OMMISSIONER GORDON'S
BEEN CALLED TO THE
MAYOR'S MANSION--
SENT US AS HIS
REPS.
WHO'S IN
CHARGE
?
RIGHT OVER THERE--
LIEUTENANT KITCH
FROM HOMICIDE.

SITUATION,
KITCH?
HE WON'T
EVEN LISTEN
TO HOSTAGE
NEGOTIATORS--
THREATENED TO
START SLITTING
THROATS IF WE
MADE ANY MOVES.
uh-huh... SO WHAT MOVES
HAVE YOU MADE?

HELLO
OUT
THERE...
BENSON--?
GOTHAM
POLICE
I'M AFRAID DEAR
BENSON IS...
DISCONNECTED
AT THE MOMENT...
AND THAT'S TWO.

WHA-BAMM

WHAT THE--?
AXTON AND
BENSON!

YOU'VE IGNORED MY
WARNING--TWICE NOW--
AND YOU KNOW WHAT
THAT MEANS!

TWO OF THE ZOMBIES--
TWO OF THE PRETTY GIRLS--
WILL HAVE TO PAY FOR YOUR
TRANSGRESSIONS!

9

BRAMBRAMBRAM
BRRRRT
KEESSH
HAHAHAHA!!
CHSH
PEESH
HOLD YOUR FIRE!!

BAMP
WE DON'T KNOW WHO MIGHT BE IN THERE -- CAN'T RISK BULLETS FLYING AROUND!
YOU GONNA SEND SOMEONE ELSE IN, KITCH?

GOT TO DO SOMETHING... BUT WE CAN'T JUST RUSH THE PLACE OR HE'LL--
NO MORE MOVES...

I'M GOING IN.
PSHAK

SOMETHIN' HINKY TO ME ABOUT THE BATMAN LATELY... LIKE HE'S HURTIN' MAYBE...

SOMETHIN' HINKY ABOUT HIM TO YOU, MONTOYA?

MONTOYA--?

TWO MORE SCARS ON ZSASZ'S SKIN-- BEFORE I EVEN GOT HERE.
GOT TO MOVE FASTER NOW-- FROM THE TOP DOWN.
HE LIKES THE DARK--FEELS SAFE IN STRIKING FROM IT...
TK

GOT TO MAKE SURE MY NIGHT VISION GEAR IS OKAY... I CAN SEE HIM-- ELIMINATE HIS ADVANTAGE...
POLITICAL SCIENCE 101
1. IRAN-CONTRA
2. BOHEMIAN GROVE
3. JFK
The UNITED STATES

NOTHING IN THE CORRIDOR... BUT HE WAS JUST UP HERE-- HURLED THE BODIES FROM--
466
SKFF
IN THERE--ZSASZ MUST HAVE HEARD OR SEEN ME--DUCKED INTO THIS OTHER CLASSROOM...
...WAITING IN AMBUSH... READY TO STRIKE WITHOUT WARNING...
BUT IF I GO IN FAST, BEFORE HE CAN--
12

IT'S... YOU?!

NOT THAT WE'VE BEEN BEST AMIGOS LATELY... KOFF... BUT I DIDN'T EXPECT US TO GO AT EACH OTHER'S THROATS LIKE--
NO TIME FOR THIS-- AND I WANT YOU TO LEAVE.
NOW.

HEY, AT LEAST LET ME TELL YOU THE NEWS I--
WE'D ONLY GET IN EACH OTHER'S WAY IN THE DARK-- AND ZSASZ IS A KILLER.

LIKE BANE'S NOT?
YOU SAW BANE?
NO... BUT I DID MEET ONE OF HIS FAITHFUL STOOGES ON--
HOW DO YOU KNOW?

HE MATCHED YOUR DESCRIPTION OF ONE OF THOSE THREE JAMOKES WHO BLASTED THE RIDDLER, OKAY?-- THE BIRD-GUY WITH HIS ATTACK-FALCON.

AND IF YOU DON'T WANT ME HERE, HOW 'BOUT I TRY TO FIND AND FOLLOW HIM?
JUST DON'T CONFRONT BANE.
LIKE THAT'S ON MY WISH LIST.

BIRD TO BANE-- BATMAN WENT IN ABOUT THREE MINUTES AGO, BUT IT'S STILL QUIET.
KEEP WATCHING.

BINGO.
13

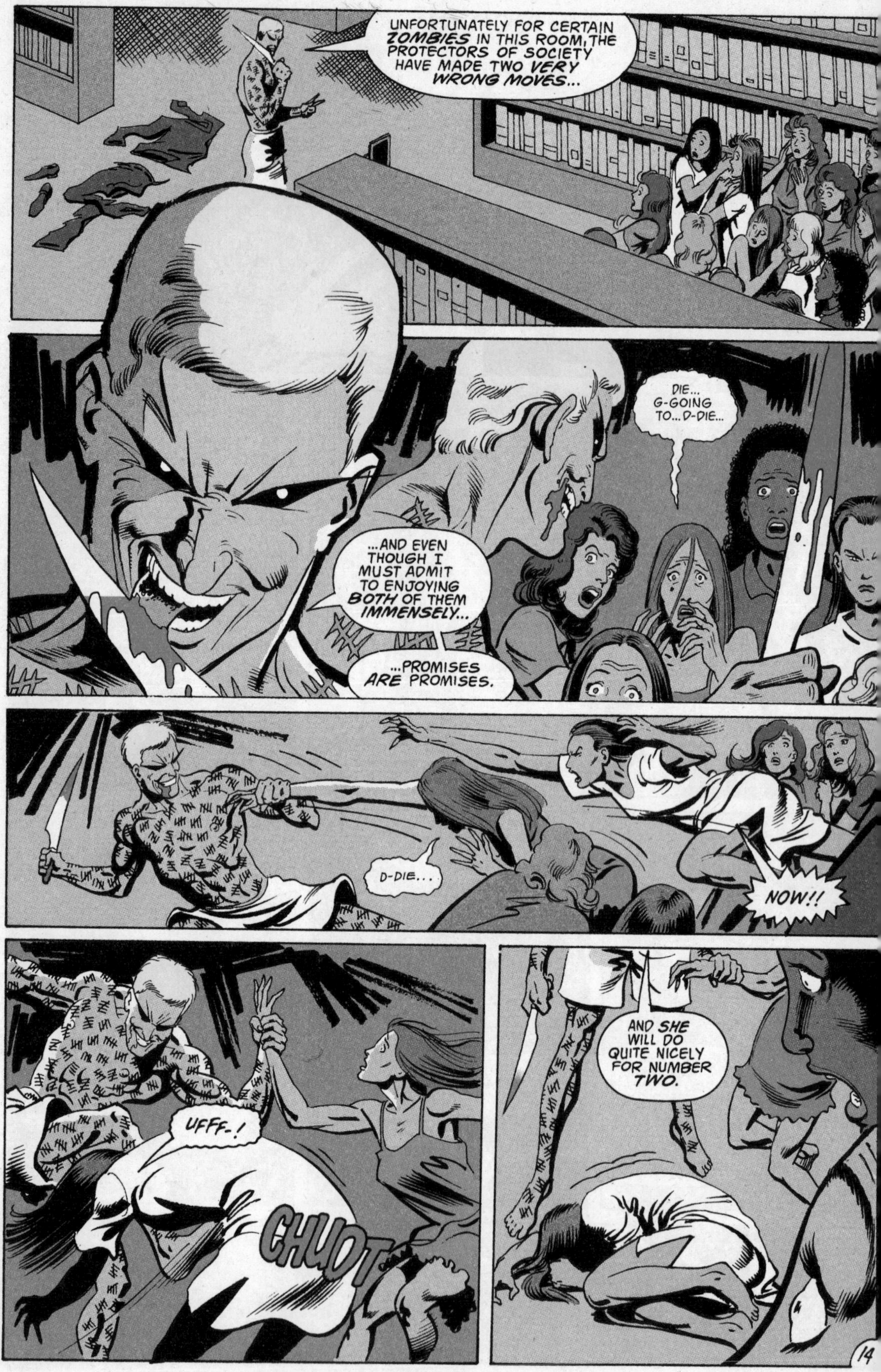

UNFORTUNATELY FOR CERTAIN *ZOMBIES* IN THIS ROOM, THE PROTECTORS OF SOCIETY HAVE MADE TWO *VERY WRONG MOVES*...

DIE... G-GOING TO... D-DIE...

...AND EVEN THOUGH I MUST ADMIT TO ENJOYING *BOTH* OF THEM *IMMENSELY*...

...PROMISES *ARE* PROMISES.

AND *SHE* WILL DO QUITE NICELY FOR NUMBER *TWO*.
14

NOW I LAY MYSELF DOWN TO SLEEP, I PRAY THE--
SHUT UP! IT'S TIME TO--
FREEZE!!
GOTHAM 115 POLICE
MONTOYA

VERY GOOD, PRETTY COP... BUT EVEN IF YOUR BULLET BEATS MY BLADE... EVEN IF IT HITS ME AND NOT THE ZOMBIE...
...DO YOU REALLY WANT TO RISK MY DEATH-TWITCH?

KROL ESTATE

--TOLD YOU YOUR MEN SHOULD SHOOT TO KILL AT THE BREAKOUT, GORDON-- BUT YOU REFUSED, AND NOW LOOK WHAT WE'VE GOT.

ONE OF MY FRIENDS HAS A DAUGHTER IN THAT SCHOOL, AND I'M HOLDING YOU PERSONALLY RESPONSIBLE.

I...

EVEN IF SHE DOESN'T GET HURT, GORDON... I THINK IT MAY WELL BE TIME FOR A NEW COMMISSIONER OF POLICE.

15

ALL RIGHT... LET HER GO... TAKE ME...
VERY NOBLE, PRETTY COP, BUT I NEED A SIGN OF GOOD FAITH...
DROP THE GUN AND TURN AROUND.
GOTHAM POLICE
AND VERY TRUSTING, PRETTY COP...
... BUT YOU'VE ONLY SAVED ONE OF THE REQUIRED TWO-- PLUS I NOW NEED ANOTHER FOR YOUR THIRD TRANSGRESSION!
HA HA HA HA HA HA HA HA HA
THAT'S ENOUGH BLOOD FOR ONE NIGHT, ZSASZ-- EVEN FOR YOU!
KLASHHH
16

I'M BETWEEN HIM AND THE HOSTAGES, BUT HE'S PIVOTING WITH MY EVERY MOVE, KEEPING MONTOYA BETWEEN US.
DON'T BARGAIN WITH HIM-- I JUST TRIED IT!
ah, BUT HE'S NOT A COP.. HE'S JUST LIKE ME-- A STALKER IN THE DARK... A FIGURE OF FEAR... A PREDATOR...

I DON'T KILL, ZSASZ.
AND YOU LOVE IT, DON'T YOU?-- ESPECIALLY WHEN YOU BRING YOUR PREY DOWN...
ah YES, YOUR "SAVING GRACE"-- THE ONE FACTOR THAT ALLOWS THE ZOMBIES TO SANCTION YOUR ACTIONS...

...THAT AND YOUR CHOICE OF VICTIMS, OF COURSE... BUT YOU'D LIKE TO KILL THEM, IF ONLY THEY'D LET YOU GET AWAY WITH IT...
...BECAUSE IT WOULD MAKE YOUR WORK SO MUCH EASIER, WOULDN'T IT?... AND EVER SO MUCH MORE SATISFYING.
YOU'RE WRONG.

AND YOU'RE DENYING! WE ARE THE SAME! WE BOTH LIKE TO COME UP ON THEM IN THE DARK, FEELING THE FORBIDDEN POWER OF IT, SEEING THE FEAR SLASHED IN THEIR FACES... WE CRAVE IT...
JUST TAKE HIM-- DON'T WORRY ABOUT ME!

TWO COPS ALREADY DOWN BECAUSE I WAS TOO SLOW, BECAUSE I'VE LOST A STEP, AND NOW... I'M NOT NEARLY FAST ENOUGH TO REACH HIM BEFORE MONTOYA GOES DOWN...
WE'RE... NOT... THE SAME.
17

Oh, THERE IS ONE DIFFERENCE! I STALK THE FRESH ONES, THE CLEAN ONES, WHILE YOU STALK THE ONES FOULED WITH BLOOD... ME AND MINE...
...SO I KNOW THE THRILL FROM BOTH SIDES...UNLIKE YOU!

BUT I SUSPECT THAT'S ALREADY BEGUN TO CHANGE, HASN'T IT?
WHAT DO YOU MEAN ?
GOTHAM POLICE
SOMEONE LOOSED THE HORDES OF ARKHAM-- ALL YOUR MOST DANGEROUS PREY-- WHICH MEANS SOMEONE HAS IT IN FOR YOU...

...SOMEONE WHO MAY BE STALKING YOU RIGHT NOW, WAITING AND WATCHING FOR JUST THE RIGHT MOMENT OF FEAR AND WEAKNESS... THE PERFECT MOMENT TO POUNCE.

I SEE I'M RIGHT... AND MAYBE YOU EVEN KNOW WHO IT IS.
AS IF YOU DON'T KNOW BANE'S NAME. WHAT'S HIS PLAN, ZSASZ? WHAT DOES HE WANT?

YOU ARE JUST LIKE ME... PARANOID... BUT IT'S THRILLING, ISN'T IT? --TO BE BOTH HUNTER AND HUNTED, KNOWING DEEP INSIDE YOU DESERVE TO BE BROUGHT DOWN...
... DOOMED TO BRING DOOM... AND DOOMED TO PAY FOR IT.

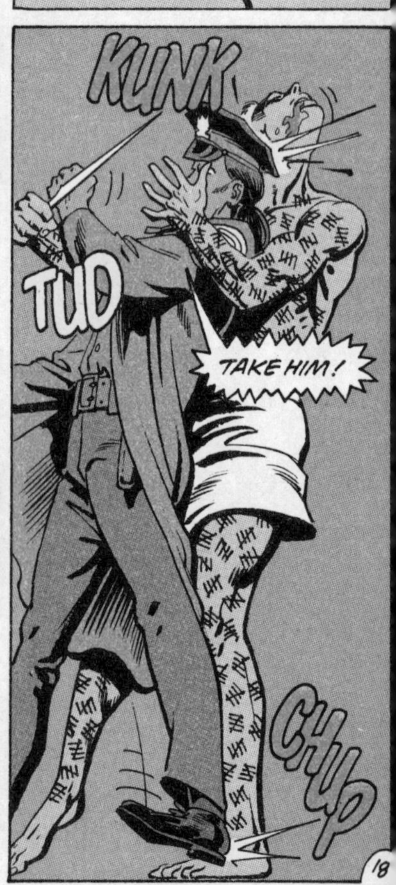

KUNK
TUD
TAKE HIM!
CHUP
18

ARE YOU ALL RIGHT?
JUST GO!
NAIL HIM!
ALREADY GONE--?
I CAN'T BE THAT SLOW..
BUT WHERE COULD ZSASZ--
NYAHRRR!!
SWUKK
SHREPT
ahn--!
BRATCH
19

HIS KNIFE--NEVER REACH HIM IN TIME...
SWFFFFFF
JUST LIKE ME--DOOMED!
YOU'RE WRONG, ZSASZ...
TCHOK
SWUMP
TUD
20

SWOK
WRONG!
KRA-KATCH
RUUUAAHHH
I'M RIGHT... AND YOU KNOW IT...
I'M ALREADY UNDER YOUR SKIN...
FINISH IT... KILL ME.
NO--!!
THRAKK
SHUT UP!!
THROKK
I'M NOT LIKE YOU, HEAR ME, KILLER?! I'M NOT LIKE --
THUNCH!
ALL RIGHT! STOP IT!!
21

THAT'S ENOUGH!
I'VE GOT HIM!

ENOUGH?
NO... TOO MUCH... WAY TOO MUCH.

IT'S OVER, BANE-- COPS ARE BRINGIN' ZSASZ OUT.
THE BATMAN DID IT AGAIN...

...BUT *THIS* TIME, *HE* LOOKS WHIPPED.

MISSED IT... BY INCHES.

BUT WHEREVER MY GRAVE IS... SOMEONE'S *STANDING* ON IT... WAITING ON IT... STOMPING THE HELL OUT OF IT.

SOMEONE NAMED BANE.

NEXT: KILLER CROC

Batman is reeling and exhausted. His encounter with Zsasz has left the Dark Knight mentally and physically drained.
Far below Gotham's streets, Robin is blindfolded and trapped between an enraged Killer Croc... And Bane...
KNIGHTFALL
4
DETECTIVE COMICS 660
by Dixon, Balent, and Hanna
DC

CROCODILE TEARS
THE EYELIDS OF MORNING.
THAT'S THE NAME GIVEN TO THE CROCODILE BY THE TRIBES THAT LIVE ALONG THE ZAMBEZI.
IT COMES FROM THE TRANSLUCENT MEMBRANE THAT COVERS THE CROCODILIAN'S EYES AND THE SHEEN THAT FLASHES ACROSS THEM...
CHUCK DIXON - writer
JIM BALENT - guest penciller
SCOTT HANNA - inker
ADRIENNE ROY - colorist
JOHN COSTANZA - letterer
SCOTT PETERSON & DENNIS O'NEIL - editors
BATMAN created by BOB KANE

...AS HE STRIKES!
REEEEEE
MORE REPTILE THAN MAN. A MIND SURRENDERED TO RAW INSTINCT AND ANIMAL DRIVE.
YESSSSSS. SO HUNGRY...
YOU'LL GO DOWN EASY... LITTLE ONE...
REEEEEE
IT WASN'T ALWAYS THIS WAY.
AND THIS ONE?
WAYLON JONES WE CALL HIM KILLER CROC. HE'S IN AND OUT OF ARKHAM MORE THAN THE KITCHEN HELP.
WHAT'S HIS STORY?
2

YOU'D NEVER KNOW IT TO *LOOK* AT HIM BUT HE RAN GOTHAM'S TOP MOB FOR A WHILE. NOW HE'S JUST ANOTHER HOPELESS NUTJOB.

HE BREAK HIS ARMS IN HERE?

NAW. THAT'S THE WAY THE COPS FOUND HIM. SOMEBODY HANDED HIM A REAL BEATING.

JEEZ. I'D HATE TO MEET *THAT* GUY.

ANY IDEA WHO RACKED HIM UP?

CROC WAS IN NO SHAPE TO TELL US. I DOUBT HE EVEN *KNOWS*.

"THAT LUNATIC LOST WHATEVER MIND HE HAD A LONG TIME AGO."

BUT HE *KNOWS*. HE KNOWS THE NAME OF THE ONE WHO HURT HIM.

BAAAAARAANE!
THE NAME THAT RUNS THROUGH HIS MIND LIKE AN ENDLESS SHRIEK.
3

IS IT WISE TO BE THIS *PUBLIC*, BANE?
AND WHAT PURPOSE DOES THE TERROR I HAVE CREATED SERVE IF I CANNOT *SAVOR* IT, ZOMBIE?
LOOK AT THE STREETS. EMPTY. LIFELESS.

A COMMUNITY COWERS BEHIND LOCKED DOORS. I HAVE CREATED A DARKNESS THAT CHILLS THEIR VERY SOULS.
I HAVE MADE A CITY INURED TO ITS OWN HORRORS KNOW FEAR.

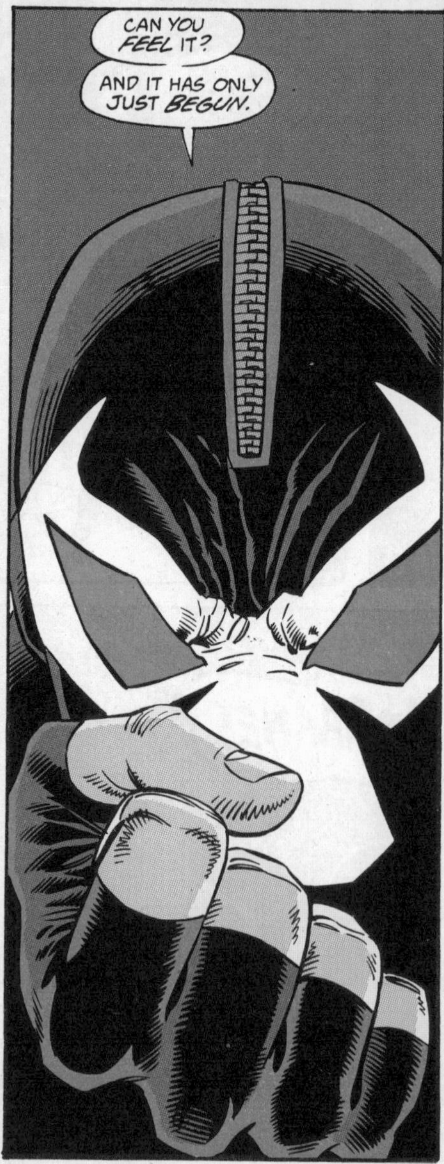
CAN YOU *FEEL* IT?
AND IT HAS ONLY JUST *BEGUN*.

AH, BIRD HAS RETURNED.
4

HE'S WHIPPED, BANE.
TELL ME MORE.
BATMAN'S AT THE END OF HIS ROPE. HE DON'T KNOW WHICH WAY TO JUMP.
HE HASN'T EVEN RUN UP AGAINST THE MAJOR LEAGUE CRAZIES THAT WE LET OUT OF ARKHAM AND ALREADY HE'S LOOKING BEAT.
WE WILL LET HIM RUN A BIT MORE OF THE GAUNTLET. I WANT TO KNOW HIS MOST EXTREME LIMITS OF ENDURANCE.
AFTER ALL, THE POINT OF THIS EXERCISE IS TO LEARN ALL I CAN ABOUT THE MAN I CAME TO GOTHAM TO DESTROY.
THE BATMAN.
THIS IS NOT GOOD.
THIS GUY'S OUT TO TAKE DOWN BATMAN AND GOTHAM CITY. AND HE'S SERIOUS ABOUT IT.
ROBIN TO BATMAN ON CLOSED CHANNEL. YOU READING ME, BATMAN? I'M STILL FOLLOWING BANE, AS WE AGREED...
5

ROBIN TO BATMAN. ARE YOU OUT THERE, BATMAN?
BATMAN, YOU'VE GOT TO COME IN...
BATMAN?
BATMAN?
BATES SCHOOL FOR GIRLS
MOVE ASIDE, COMIN' THROUGH.
MMPH. URGH.
YOU JUST KEEP RIGHT ON STARIN' HOLES IN ME, ZSASZ. I BEEN EYE-BUGGED BY BETTER THAN YOU.
WE GOT A NICE LITTLE CELL WAITIN' FOR YOU,
AND YOU BETTER STAY THERE, PAL, 'CAUSE THE NEXT TIME YOU GET OUT I'LL MAKE SURE THERE'S NO OTHER COPS AROUND.
JUST YOU, AND ME, AND SMITH AND WESSON.
I'D DO YOU RIGHT HERE AND NOW BUT I DON'T WANT TO SPEND THE REST OF MY TWENTY TALKING TO INTERNAL AFFAIRS HUMPS.
6

"BESIDES, I GOT A LOT OF OTHER LOONIES TO LOOK FOR."
MR. DETWEILER...?
MR. DETWEILER, ATTORNEY AT LAW...?
WHUZZ?
WHAH?
WHAT IS THIS? WHO ARE YOU?
YOU CAN CALL ME SOCKO, COUNSELOR. AND YOU ALREADY KNOW YOUR VALUED CLIENT, THE VENTRILOQUIST.
WHAT DO YOU WANT?

YOU WERE THE LAST TO DEFEND MY PAL AND HIS GUDDY SCARFACE. WE WANT TO KNOW WHERE SCARFACE GOT TO.
THIS IS ALL ABOUT THAT STUPID PUPPET? YOU'RE NUTS. WHY SHOULD I HELP YOU FIND ANYTHING?

'CAUSE GULLETS MAKE NASTY HOLES.
"DARNED IF YOU DO, DARNED IF YOU DON'T." THAT'S SOCK HUMOR, COUNSELOR.
7

FLANDERS. HE'S HERE TO TRY AND MAKE SENSE OF THIS WHOLE ARKHAM SITUATION.
HARRY MANN SHOW
WE'VE GOT A CITY PARALYZED WITH FEAR. THE STREETS ARE FULL OF WACKOS WITH ASSAULT WEAPONS. AND YOU THINK YOU'VE GOT THE SOLUTION?
I DO, HARRY.
YOU SEE, ALL OF THIS PANIC AND STRESS HAS CREATED A HOSTILE ENVIRONMENT FOR THE INMATES.
FEAR FEEDS ON FEAR AND ONLY SERVES TO MAKE MATTERS WORSE.
YOU'RE SAYING THAT BY BEING AFRAID OF AN ARMY OF HOMICIDAL MANIACS LOOSE ON OUR STREETS WE'RE ANTAGONIZING THEM?
EXACTLY. AS DETAILED IN MY BOOK, "I'M SANE AND SO ARE YOU," THE MENTALLY DIVERGENT SHOULD BE MADE TO FEEL AT EASE IN OUR ENVIRONMENT.
A CLIMATE OF MISTRUST AND SUSPICION ONLY TENDS TO MAKE THEM FEEL INSECURE IN THEIR CHOICE OF LIFESTYLES.
I'M SANE AND SO ARE YOU
WE'VE GOT A BODY COUNT HEADING TOWARD THE TRIPLE DIGITS.
THAT'S A "LIFE-STYLE"?
8

"YOU'RE DANGEROUS, DOC."
ANYTHING ELSE TO REPORT TO ME, BIRD?
WELL, I THINK YOU SHOULD'VE LET ME WASTE THAT ROBIN BRAT. THAT KID COULD GET TO BE A PAIN.
NO. WE WILL DISPOSE OF THE BOY LATER. IF YOU WANT THE JOB IT IS YOURS.
BUT FOR NOW HE MAY PROVE USEFUL.
MAN...
CAN'T SAY I CARE FOR THIS CONVERSATION.
I WANT YOU ALL TO CONTINUE YOUR SURVEILLANCE.
ALL OF US?
YES, TROGG. EVENTS WILL MOVE SWIFTLY FROM HERE. I WANT COMPLETE COVERAGE OF THE BATMAN'S DECLINE.
I WILL NEED TO DECIDE THE PRECISE MOMENT AT WHICH I SHOULD MAKE MY FINAL MOVE.
REMAIN IN RADIO CONTACT!
SO, WHAT DO I DO NOW?
9

WISH I COULD GET BATMAN ON THE RADIO.
I'D BETTER KEEP UP WITH THIS GUY UNTIL I CAN.
SOUNDS LIKE HIM AND HIS BUDDIES ARE THE ONES WHO BUSTED ARKHAM OPEN.
THIS IS DEFINITELY ONE TO KEEP AN EYE ON.
I HAVE THE FEELING EVERYTHING I'VE DONE SO FAR HAS BEEN PRACTICE.
10

HEADING INTO THE SUBWAY. NO WAY I CAN RADIO BATMAN THROUGH ALL THAT CONCRETE AND STEEL.
PROBABLY OUT OF RANGE BY NOW.

STARLITE LENS WILL HELP ME KEEP AN EYE ON TALL, DARK AND GRUESOME.

WAIT A MINUTE...
DID HE FALL OFF?

NOW *THERE'S* A HAPPY THOUGHT. OUR MYSTERY VILLAIN DONE IN BY THE SHELDON PARK "D" TRAIN.

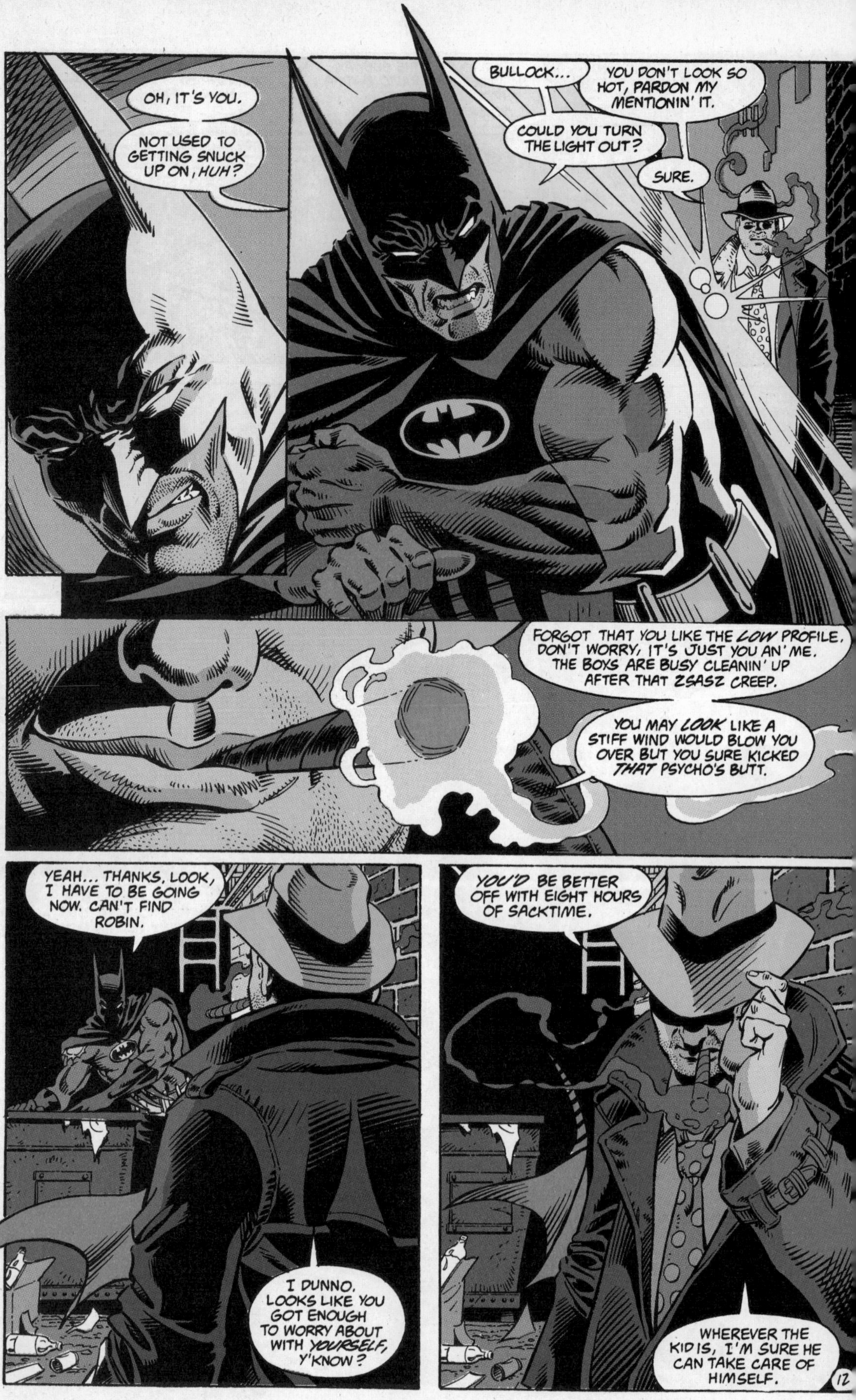

OH, IT'S YOU.
NOT USED TO GETTING SNUCK UP ON, *HUH?*
BULLOCK...
YOU DON'T LOOK SO HOT, PARDON MY MENTIONIN' IT.
COULD YOU TURN THE LIGHT OUT?
SURE.
FORGOT THAT YOU LIKE THE *LOW* PROFILE. DON'T WORRY, IT'S JUST YOU AN' ME. THE BOYS ARE BUSY CLEANIN' UP AFTER THAT ZSASZ CREEP.
YOU MAY *LOOK* LIKE A STIFF WIND WOULD BLOW YOU OVER BUT YOU SURE KICKED *THAT* PSYCHO'S BUTT.

YEAH... THANKS. LOOK, I HAVE TO BE GOING NOW. CAN'T FIND ROBIN.
I DUNNO. LOOKS LIKE YOU GOT ENOUGH TO WORRY ABOUT WITH *YOURSELF,* Y'KNOW?

YOU'D BE BETTER OFF WITH EIGHT HOURS OF SACKTIME.
WHEREVER THE KID IS, I'M SURE HE CAN TAKE CARE OF HIMSELF.
12

"WHICH IS BETTER ODDS THAN I'D GIVE YOU RIGHT NOW."
DON'T LIKE THIS.
CAN'T SEE WHERE I AM.
CAN HEAR WATER RUSHING. LOTS OF WATER.
ECHOES. I'M IN A LARGE, ENCLOSED SPACE.
BREATHING... WHO--?
I AM VERY CURIOUS ABOUT YOU. YOU AID THE BATMAN IN HIS FIGHT AGAINST CRIME, EH?
AND YET YOU ARE JUST A BOY.
I AM JUST BEGINNING TO UNDERSTAND YOUR MENTOR. BUT YOU ARE A WILD CARD TO ME.
WHERE HAVE I HEARD THAT BEFORE?
YOUR NAME IS BANE, ISN'T IT?
13

AND THE OTHER ONE? THE ONE WHO PRETENDED TO BE THE BATMAN?
JUST ANOTHER ONE OF OUR MERRY MEN.
YOU KNOW I WENT TO THE TROUBLE OF BLINDFOLDING YOU.
IT WOULD HAVE BEEN MUCH EASIER TO SIMPLY BLIND YOU.
BUT I APPRECIATE YOUTHFUL DEFIANCE. YOU STRUGGLE AGAINST YOUR FEAR. I ADMIRE THAT.
REALLY? MAYBE I'LL CALL YOU IF I EVER NEED A JOB REFERENCE.
THIS GUY IS A WORLD-CLASS SICKY. I'VE GOT TO GET AWAY FROM HIM AND FREE MY HANDS.
NO ROOM TO MOVE. WHERE ARE WE?
YOU MAY BE USEFUL TO ME YET. I IMAGINE THAT THE BATMAN WOULD COME TO HELP YOU IF HE KNEW YOU WERE IN DANGER.
FORGET IT, BANE.
I'M NO HOSTAGE. BATMAN'S NOT GOING TO FALL INTO ANY TRAPS FOR MY SAKE.
SUCH BRAVE WORDS. SUCH CAMARADERIE. BUT YOU MAY BE RIGHT.
14

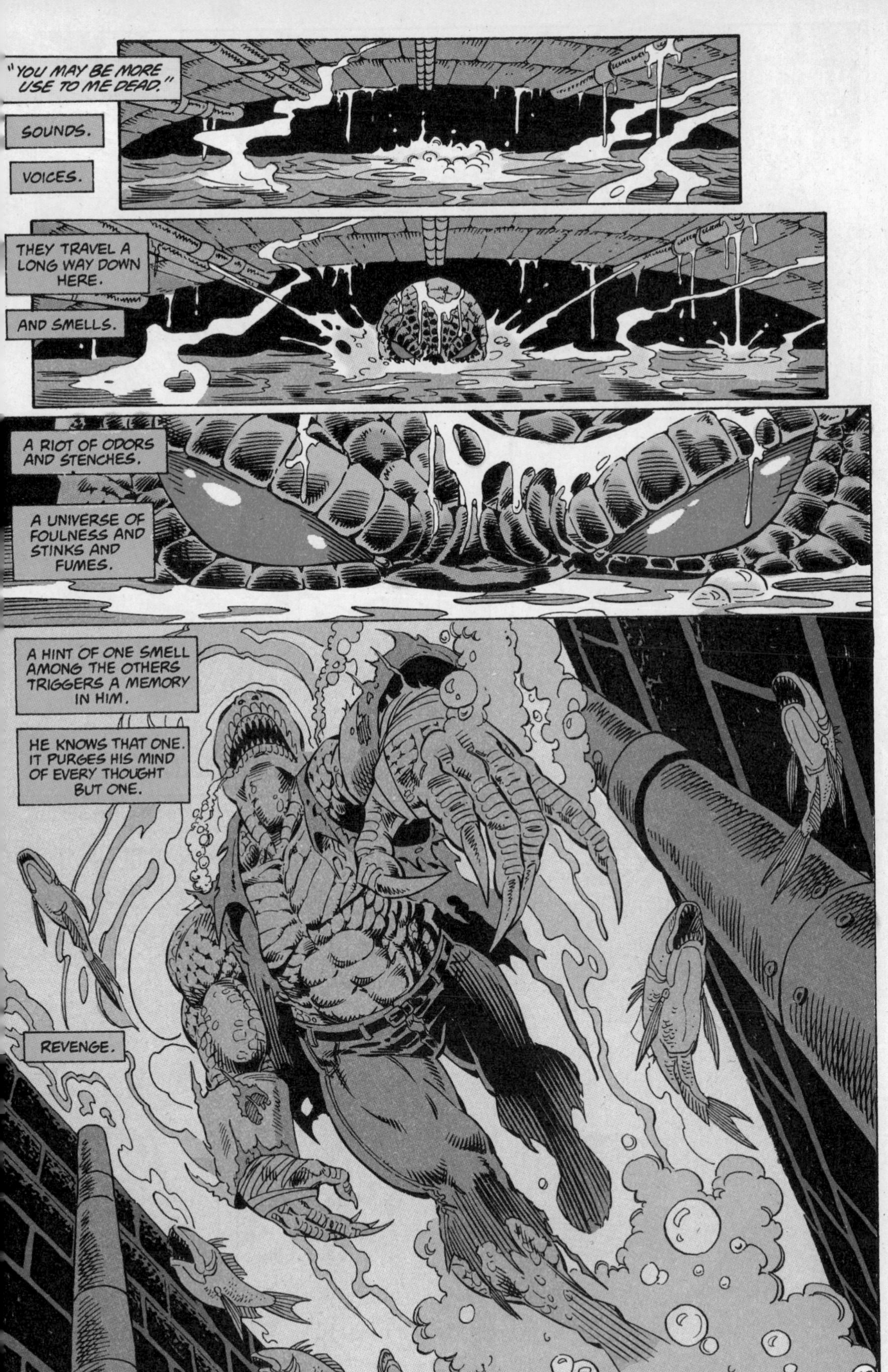
"YOU MAY BE MORE USE TO ME DEAD."
SOUNDS.
VOICES.
THEY TRAVEL A LONG WAY DOWN HERE.
AND SMELLS.
A RIOT OF ODORS AND STENCHES.
A UNIVERSE OF FOULNESS AND STINKS AND FUMES.
A HINT OF ONE SMELL AMONG THE OTHERS TRIGGERS A MEMORY IN HIM.
HE KNOWS THAT ONE. IT PURGES HIS MIND OF EVERY THOUGHT BUT ONE.
REVENGE.
15

THIS IS HOPELESS. I CAN'T GET A FIX ON HIM WITH ALL THIS NOISE.
I AM GROWING IMPATIENT.
REALLY?
CAN'T JUST LET THIS LUNATIC KILL ME.
I CAN'T TELL YOU HOW SORRY I AM ABOUT THAT.
THIS BEGINS TO BORE ME.
THERE'S SO MUC YOU COULD TELL M ABOUT THE BATMA I HAVE NO REAL DESIRE TO KILL YOU.
UNLESS YOU CAUSE TROUBLE FOR ME.
TELL ME ABOUT MY ENEMY. TELL ME EVERYTHING I NEED AND I WILL RELEASE YOU.
I'LL TELL YOU ONE THING, BANE...
HE'S BEATEN GUYS WHO MAKE YOU LOOK LIKE A GIRL SCOUT.
THAT RIGHT. SA SOMETHIN TO MAKE HIM MAD.

REAL BRIGHT MOVE, BOY WONDER.
UNNH!
I HAVE NO TIME FOR THIS!
YOU WILL BE--
SOMEONE COMING.
YOU CAN THREATEN ME ALL YOU WANT BUT IT'S NOT GOING TO HELP YOU AGAINST BATMAN, BANE.
BANE?
I KNOW YOU'RE STILL HERE, BANE.
YOU REALLY SHOULD DO SOMETHING ABOUT THE MOUTH BREATHING.
HUH?
WHERE IS HE?
17

WAS IT CROC ALL ALONG?
WHERE IS HE?
I--I DON'T KNOW WHERE BATMAN IS.
NOT HIM...
NO WAY. CROC'S NOT ONE FOR MINDGAMES.
THE ONE CALLED BANE! THE ONE WHO BROKE MY ARMS!
THE STINK OF HIM IS EVERY-WHERE!
THIS IS NO PLACE FOR A ROBIN.
UNNH!
18

I THOUGHT I HAD BROKEN YOU, ANIMALE.
NOT ENOUGH, I SUPPOSE.
NOW I WILL HAVE TO KILL YOU.
WOCK!
YEAH? WELL, YOU'RE GONNA HAVE TO DO IT...
SHRISH
...WITHOUT YER SECRET WEAPON, PAL!
I'M A LOSER NO MATTER WHO WINS.
HAVE TO GET... MY HANDS... FREE...
19

HANDS ARE NUMB.
CAN'T DO...IT.
YOU HAVE TO.
THIS ISN'T A... GAME...
YOU FREE YOURSELF... OR YOU'RE...
DEAD.
YES!
NOT SO HOT WITHOUT YOUR JUICE, ARE YA, BANE?
YA WANT T'BE TOP MAN IN GOTHAM, HUH?
YOU AIN'T EVEN A CONTENDER!
SKRUNCH
20

I DON'T NEED VENOM TO KILL AN INSECT LIKE YOU.
I AM BANE!
ARRRRRRRRR
THE BANE OF ANYTHING THAT GETS IN MY WAY!
THE BANE OF ANYTHING THAT LIVES!
KRUNK!
OH, MAN...
THIS ARCH WASN'T BUILT FOR HEAVY-WEIGHT GRUDGE MATCHES. THIS WHOLE THING IS GOING TO...
FALL!
21

AT LEAST MY HANDS ARE FREE.
GOOD BOY, TIM. LOOK ON THE SUNNY SIDE.

THE TWO UGLIES ARE TOO INTENT ON EACH OTHER TO BOTHER WITH ME.
SMALL FAVORS.

STILL THAT LITTLE PROBLEM OF DROWNING.
CURRENT'S TOO STRONG TO FIGHT.

TUNNELS RUN DEEPER INTO THE SYSTEM.
MAYBE TO GOTHAM HARBOR.

GUESS I'M GOING TO FIND OUT HOW LONG I CAN HOLD MY BREATH.
TO BE CONTINUED IN KNIGHTFALL PART 5

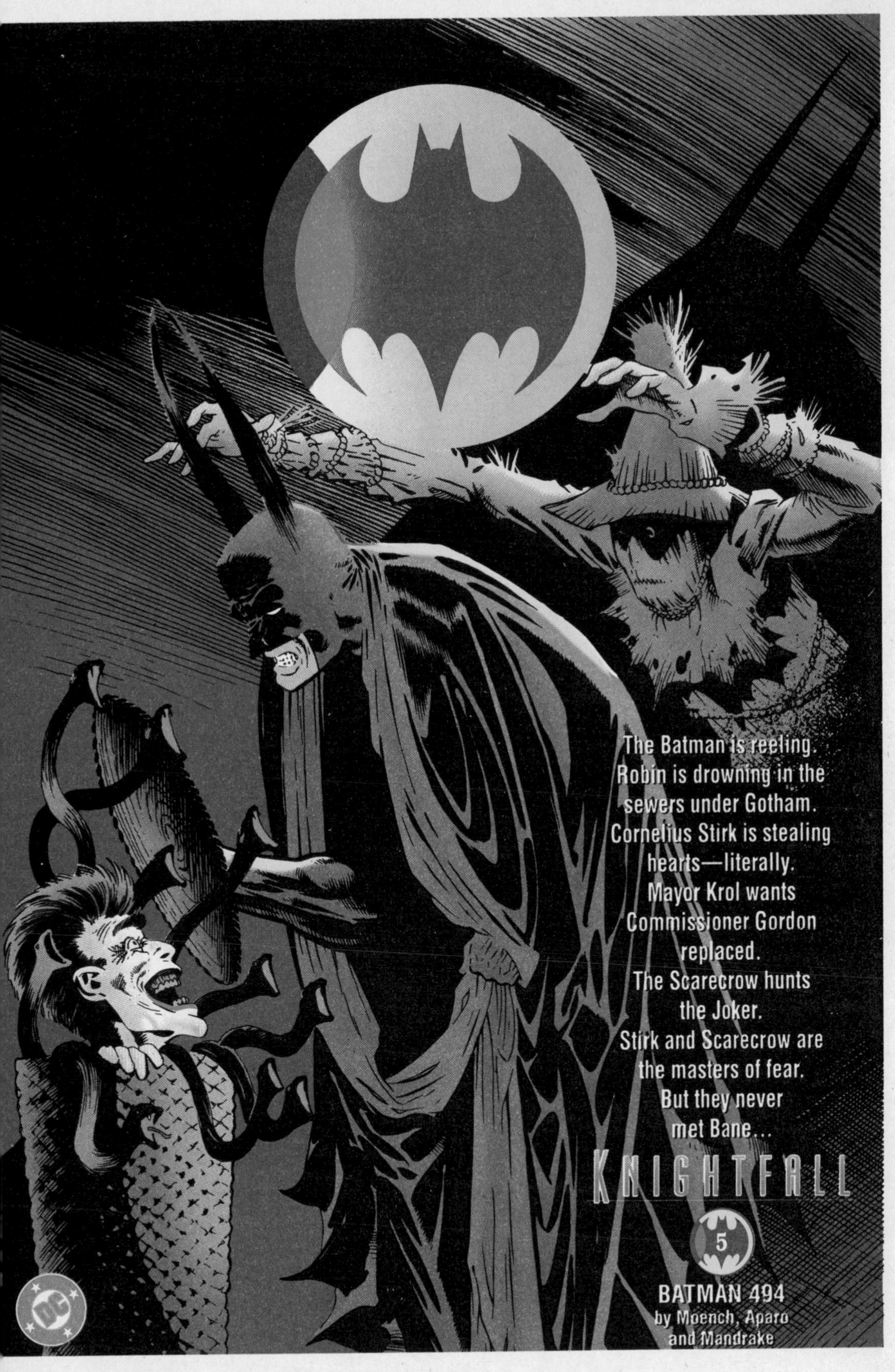
The Batman is reeling.
Robin is drowning in the sewers under Gotham.
Cornelius Stirk is stealing hearts—literally.
Mayor Krol wants Commissioner Gordon replaced.
The Scarecrow hunts the Joker.
Stirk and Scarecrow are the masters of fear.
But they never met Bane...
KNIGHTFALL
5
BATMAN 494
by Moench, Aparo and Mandrake
DC

THE GOTHAM SEWERS:
CURRENT'S TOO STRONG -- SWEEPING ME TOWARD THE OUTFLOW TUNNELS -- ALL THE WAY TO GOTHAM HARBOR...
...A DESTINATION THAT'LL DEFINITELY LEAVE ME BREATHLESS.
NIGHT TERRORS
BATMAN CREATED BY BOB KANE
DOUG MOENCH WRITER
JIM APARO PENCILLER
TOM MANDRAKE INKER
ADRIENNE ROY COLORIST
RICHARD STARKINGS LETTERER
JORDAN B. GORFINKEL ASST. EDITOR
DENNY O'NEIL EDITOR

GOTTA FIGHT TO THE SURFACE -- FAST..!
CHAKT
SNK
Huhhhh
...AND PIN MY LAST HOPE ON THE STAFF...
SNK
DID IT! -- BUT IF I CAN'T SUCK UP ENOUGH STRENGTH FOR THE NEXT STEP...
...I'LL JUST DROWN HERE INSTEAD OF HALFWAY THROUGH THE TUNNEL...
THIS IS IT -- TIME FOR THE LAST-GASP EFFORT...
2

...NOW!
FWNT
WP
WP WP
CHNK
BINGO! AND SO MUCH FOR THAT TRUSTY STAFF OF LIFE...
SPSH
"...AT LEAST I DON'T HAVE TO WORRY ABOUT BANE AND KILLER CROC ANYMORE...
"... BUT, SOMEHOW, THAT PARTICULAR SILVER LINING...
"...LACKS A CERTAIN SHIMMER AND SPARKLE..."
...STILL, JUST LEMME OUTTA HERE...
...AND I'LL TAKE IT!
3

THE HUB:

EXCUSE ME, SIR, JUST A MOMENT...

...WHILE I STIR THE SOUP.

Mmm... AND A **HEARTY BROTH** IT *IS*, SIR, FLAVORED JUST AS I *LIKE* IT, WITH ALL THE BLOOD'S MOMENT-OF-DEATH **FEAR**, HEAVY ON NOREPINEPHRINE AND --

TOK TOK

WHO *IS* IT?

JOE.

JOE **WHO?**

WAYNE MANOR:
--AFRAID I'LL HAVE TO CANCEL MY APPOINTMENT AGAIN.
FOR THE FIFTH TIME?!
I KNOW, DOCTOR KINSOLVING, BUT --

I TOLD YOU TO CALL ME SHONDRA, BRUCE, BUT IF YOU'RE NOT EVEN GOING TO GIVE MY TREATMENT A FAIR CHANCE --
BELIEVE ME, SHONDRA, A GENUINE EMERGENCY HAS COME UP, A WHOLE SCORE OF EMER--
SIR--!

IT'S MASTER TIM, SIR -- DOWN-STAIRS!
SORRY, SHONDRA-- I'LL CALL YOU!

BAKK KLIK
AGAIN... AND IT FEELS LIKE A PERSONAL REJECTION ... JUST LIKE THE OTHER TIMES...

... BUT WHY?
WHY AM I SO CONCERNED ABOUT THIS ONE PARTICULAR PATIENT ABOVE ALL OTHERS?
WHY AM I REACTING TO HIM... AS IF HE'S BECOMING MORE THAN A PATIENT?
5

THE MAYOR'S MANSION:
--ENTIRE SITUATION HAS BEEN MISHANDLED FROM THE BEGINNING, GORDON -- FROM THE FIRST MOMENT THE ARKHAM BREAK-OUT BEGAN!
AND IF YOU DON'T DO SOMETHING ABOUT IT WITHIN TWENTY-FOUR HOURS, I'M GOING TO ASK THE GOVERNOR TO CALL OUT THE NATIONAL GUARD!
BUT, IF YOU DO THAT--
THAT'S RIGHT, GORDON...
THE MAYOR OF THIS CITY WIELDS IMMENSE POWER, AND WITH THE PUBLICITY SURROUNDING A SINGLE PHONE CALL...
--I CAN DESTROY YOUR CAREER.
THE CAVE:
--SURE YOU'RE ALL RIGHT?
ME? WHAT ABOUT YOU, MAN?
STAY HUNCHED OVER, TIMOTHY...

I ONLY TOOK A BRIEF DIP IN THE SEWERS--
BREATHE THE VAPORS.
--BUT YOU'VE BEEN WALLOWING NONSTOP IN HELL.
DON'T WORRY ABOUT ME -- I KNOW WHERE I'VE BEEN, AND IT'S ONLY THE BEGINNING.

THERE ARE MANIACS TO STOP -- AND BANE'S INTENTIONS TO LEARN.
WHY WOULD HE AND KILLER CROC TRY TO KILL EACH OTHER -- AFTER HE BROKE CROC OUT OF ARKHAM? IS THE PLAN GOING SOUR?

MAYBE THERE IS NO MASTER PLAN.
GOT TO BE.
HEY, HE ALSO BUSTED THE RIDDLER OUT OF ARKHAM, DIDN'T HE--? AFTER HIS THREE STOOGES TRIED TO WASTE RIDDLER WITH AUTOMATIC WEAPONS...
TOO RANDOM FOR SOMEONE AS CALCULATING AS BANE...
SO MAYBE THE PURPOSE BEHIND THE ARKHAM BREAK-OUT WAS NOTHING BUT CHAOS -- OR AT MOST A PLAN TO CREATE DIVERSIONS ALL OVER THE PLACE, AND WITH YOU LESS THAN ONE-HUNDRED PER CENT --

BESIDES, THE RIDDLER WAS ALL PUMPED UP -- FROM THE SAME VENOM BANE IS APPARENTLY USING, WHICH MEANS BANE ENHANCED THE RIDDLER BEFORE HIS THREE ACCOMPLICES TRIED TO KILL HIM...
...IF THEY ARE HIS ACCOM-PLICES.

THEY ARE -- OR AT LEAST THE BIRD-GUY IS -- I HEARD 'EM COMMUNICATING BY RADIO.
AND MAYBE THE RANDOM-NESS IS THE PLAN.
7

I STILL DON'T BUY IT, ROBIN.
AT THE VERY LEAST, BANE IS USING THE ARKHAM INMATES HE FREED -- FOR A DELIBERATE PURPOSE.
RIGHT-- AND HE'S USING THEM TO DESTROY YOU --!
THAT'S THE PURPOSE -- AND YOU CAN'T FALL FOR IT!
WHAT'S THE ALTERNATIVE, ROBIN? LETTING MADNESS RUN ROUGHSHOD OVER GOTHAM?
I TOLD YOU WHAT ZSASZ DID!
HEY, I KNOW THE SITUATION, BUT YOU NEED A REST.
MAYBE IF AZRAEL AND I --
JEAN-PAUL IS FORMIDABLE -- MAYBE EVEN UP TO THE TASK...
BUT BANE IS AFTER ME -- AND AS LONG AS I CAN STAND, THIS IS MY BUSINESS.
ALFRED... THIS IS NUTS.
INDEED.
IN MY CONSIDERED OPINION, YOU ARE BOTH BEYOND HOPE.

THE HOTEL SUITE:
AND YOU DIDN'T SEE CROC AGAIN?
NOT AFTER WE WERE WASHED FROM THE TUNNEL...

BUT FORGET KILLER CROC -- OUR REAL PREY IS COMING UP NOW...
--TENSE HOSTAGE CRISIS AT THE BATES SCHOOL FOR WOMEN ENDED ONLY WHEN THE BATMAN ALLEGEDLY PUT AN END TO ZSASZ'S RAMPAGE OF TERROR...

...BUT OUR EXCLUSIVE INTERVIEWS WITH SEVERAL OF THE STUDENTS FOLLOWING THEIR HARROWING ORDEAL INDICATE THAT THE BATMAN SEEMED SOMEHOW DEBILITATED BY THE ENCOUNTER...

...AS IF ZSASZ MAY HAVE PSYCHOLOGICALLY AFFECTED THE DARK KNIGHT DETECTIVE...
SO WHAT? HE STILL SUCCEEDED -- PUT ANOTHER ONE BACK IN ARKHAM.
BUT NOW THE EROSION IS TOUCHING HIS MIND, BIRD, AS WELL AS HIS BODY.

THE PLAN IS WORKING.
THE BATMAN IS REELING... READY TO FALL.

YOUR VENOM-FEED, BANE -- GOOD AS NEW.
THANK YOU, ZOMBIE... I COULD USE A JOLT RIGHT NOW.
9

THE STREETS:
ZSASZ TAUGHT ME A BITTER LESSON -- HOW FAST AN INSANE MURDERER CAN STRIKE -- MUCH LIKE ANOTHER SERIAL KILLER RECENTLY ESCAPED FROM ARKHAM...
CORNELIUS STIRK.
COMPUTER SEARCH -- HISTORICAL FIGURES -- ANOMALOUS REPORTS--
--WITHIN LAST WEEK.
SEARCHING.
JOHN FITZGERALD KENNEDY SEEN AT ASHBURN AND OAK CLIFF; MAHATMA GANDHI REPORTED ON SEWELL NEAR RAVENSWOOD; ELVIS PRESLEY SIGHTED AT--
ENOUGH.
THE KENNEDY AND GANDHI LOCATIONS ARE BOTH IN THE HUB, EXACTLY THE KIND OF NEIGHBORHOOD FAVORED BY STIRK -- AND SINCE HE'S USED HIS HYPNOTIC POWERS TO APPEAR AS ABRAHAM LINCOLN IN THE PAST...
SKREEERAOW
THE HUB IT IS!
10

SOUTHTOWN:
THE 8 BALL
POOL
POOL BILLI
HUUAHHH!
KRESSH
WHAT THE--?!
YOU! YOU'VE WORKED FOR THE JOKER IN THE PAST, HAVEN'T YOU?
WHERE IS HE?!
SKSHSH
N-N-NOT HERE... S-SAID HE MIGHT N-NEED ME L-LATER...
W-WHAT, WHAT DID YOU S-S-SQUIRT AT ME?
FEAR.
11

P-PLEASE... I... I'M TERRIFIED OF HEIGHTS...

YOUR GREATEST FEAR... YOUR MOST PROMINENT PHOBIA... CHEMICALLY INDUCED...

...AND THERE'S A LOT MORE WHERE IT CAME FROM IF YOU DON'T TALK!

WHY MIGHT THE JOKER NEED YOU LATER? WHAT FOR? WHAT'S HE UP TO?

K-KIDNAP AND C-CONTROL COMMISSIONER GORDON... USE HIM TO... F-FOUL UP THE WHOLE... P-POLICE FORCE... SO W-WE CAN DO WHATEVER WE W-WANT...

...BUT P-PLEASE... IF THESE POOLCUES B-BREAK...

KRATCH
12

YAAAAAAAAAAAAAA
THANKS FOR THE INFORMATION.
AND SWEET DREAMS.
THE HUB:
THE SMELL OF BLOOD... DECAY...
NEARBY.
TOO LATE -- AGAIN...
STIRK! HIS CART -- USED FOR THE DISPOSAL OF HIS VICTIMS BODIES--!
SKWEE SKWEE SKWEE SKWEE
13

SKWEE BUMP SKWEE
THERE --!
--IT'S HIM!
HIS NEW PLACE!
STIRK!

THE APARTMENT OF JEAN-PAUL VALLEY:
-- GETTING WORRIED ABOUT HIM, PAUL... REAL WORRIED...

... AND EVEN IF HE DOESN'T WANT US, I'VE GOT A BAD FEELING HE'LL NEED US.
I'LL BE READY, ROBIN.

I SWEAR IT.

POLICE HQ:
OVER HERE, GORDON.
ABOUT TIME --

-- THOUGHT YOU'D NEVER ANSWER THE SIGNAL.
MAYOR KROL'S THREATENING TO CALL OUT THE NATIONAL GUARD...
IT'D MEAN LOSING MY JOB... RIGHT AFTER SARAH AND I JUST GOT MARRIED...
AND IF I LEAVE AS POLICE COMMISSIONER... IT'D PROBABLY MEAN THE END OF YOU TOO.
15

I DOUBT IT, SIR!

SNOKK

GUH-H!

AND, IN ANY CASE, SUCH A PALE AND POOR APPREHENSION, COMMISSIONER... WHEN THE RICHNESS OF UNBRIDLED FEAR KNOWS NO BOUNDS...

WH-WHAT ARE YOU--

FEAR IS OUR GREATEST FRIEND, SIR...

...AND WHO IS YOUR GREATEST FRIEND?

Y-YOU... YOU'RE NOT--

THAT'S RIGHT, SIR -- I'M NOT! I'M REALLY THE MAN WHO NEEDS YOUR FRESHLY HARVESTED HEART...

...ITS NOREPINEPHRINE AND ADRENALIN... ITS DELICIOUSLY BUBBLING STRESS HORMONES... ALL THE NATURAL INGREDIENTS FOR A STEW OF ORGANIC FEAR...

NO, YOU MORON!

YOU WERE SUPPOSED TO KIDNAP -- NOT KILL HIM!
16

FEAR, SIR! FEAR AND ALL IT BRINGS!
FEAR'S PUNGENT--
TANG
GET AWAY FROM HIM, GORDON!
WHOEVER YOU'RE SEEING, HE'S REALLY CORNELIUS STIRK!
S-STIRK?
BRAMM
FWWT
EXHAUSTED -- TIMING'S OFF -- MISSED THE GUN...
OOPPH!
CHUFT
AND NOW BATS SHOWS UP!
WHAT AN UNMITIGATED DISASTER!
17

SWUK
THRAK
SHUMP
CHATT
FYAH! NEVER SHOULD'VE USED STIRK! TOO UNSTABLE! AFTER ALL, HE'S CRAZY!
INDEED...
Eh?
SKAT

AFTER MY VISIT TO THE 8-BALL, I KNEW I'D FIND YOU SOMEWHERE NEAR GORDON...
SCARECROW -- WHAT A BIZARRE SURPRISE!
...AND I'M OFFENDED, JOKER, BY THE FACT THAT YOU WENT TO A RANK AMATEUR IN THE REALM OF FEAR...
...WHEN THE MASTER WAS READILY AVAIL-ABLE.

MEANING YOU, OF COURSE... BUT MAYBE I FIGURED I COULD CONTROL STIRK, Eh?
AND HOW WRONG YOU WERE! BAD CHOICE, JOKER -- AND IT MAKES ME ANGRY.
IN FACT, I'M TEMPTED TO GIVE YOU A DOSE OF MY FEAR...

HAHAHA
JUST TRY IT, SCARECROW! I'M SURE I'D FIND THE EXPERIENCE HIGHLY AMUSING!
I'D PREFER TAKING STIRK'S PLACE -- BUT THIS TIME IT MUST BE AN EQUAL PARTNER-SHIP...
NO ONE CONTROLS ANYONE.

JUST WHAT DO YOU HAVE IN MIND..? IF ONE MAY USE THE TERM ON CRANIUM-PACKED STRAW.
THE POLICE COMMISSIONER IS PEANUTS! IF YOU WANT TO BRING REAL FEAR AND CHAOS TO GOTHAM...
...WHY NOT GO STRAIGHT TO THE TOP?
TERROR-IZE THE MAYOR?
Hmm... I THINK... I LIKE IT!
HAHAHA
19

R-RED GRID... MANDALA... OF B-BLOOD...
EASY, GORDON -- IT'S JUST AN HYPNOTIC MIND-PLANT... HIS PSIONIC POWER PUT YOU INTO A --
RED GRIIIIIID!! BATMAN KILLED MEEEE!!
JAMES!
MY GOD, WHAT HAVE YOU DONE TO HIM!?!
IT... IT WAS CORNELIUS STIRK... POSING AS ME...
STIRK? THE SERIAL KILLER?
B-BATMAN... MY F-FRIEND... WITH A KNIFE...
IF IT WEREN'T FOR YOU --
YOU'RE WRONG, MRS. GORDON -- YOUR HUSBAND WAS THE TARGET, NOT ME.
JUST AS HE WAS IN THE HEADHUNTER INCIDENT --
--WHEN I TOLD YOU TO LEAVE US ALONE?!

EVERYTHING EXPLODING... CRUMBLING... COLLAPSING...

...AND THE BIG ONES... THE ONES LIKE TWO-FACE AND THE JOKER...
THEY HAVEN'T EVEN MADE THEIR MOVES YET!

THE MAYOR'S MANSION, MASTER BEDROOM:
FSSSSSSSSSSSSSSSS
NFFF... MMNN? ?
HAHAHAHAHAHAHA
BWAMM
?! WHA?!
N-NO! C-CAN'T BE REAL--!
M-MUST BE ... A N-NIGHTMARE... N-NOT REAL..!
Ah... BUT WE ARE VERY REAL INDEED, MR. MAYOR... HYPER-REAL...
"...AS YOUR BODYGUARDS DOWNSTAIRS COULD READILY ATTEST -- WERE THEY STILL CAPABLE OF SPEECH."
N-NO... P-P-POISONOUS!
WHAT'S POISONOUS, MR. MAYOR? WHAT ARE YOU SEEING? WHAT'S YOUR GREATEST FEAR?
SPIDERS? SNAKES?
BAD SUSHI?
21

S-SNAKES
P-P-POISONOUS...
SNAKES, MR. MAYOR... SERPENTS, VIPERS -- THEIR FORKED TONGUES FLICKERING, TICKLING THE SOFT THROBBING FLESH OF YOUR THROAT, GREASING THE WAY FOR THE SWIFT SHOCKING PUNCTURE OF HOOKED...
HOLLOW...
FANGS!
SSSSS! THIS IS WONDERFUL, SCARECROW-- FABULOUS!
P-P-PLEASE.. WH-WHAT... WHAT DO YOU W-WANT?
IT'S TIME TO EXERCISE YOUR CITY-WIDE INFLUENCE, MR. MAYOR... AS YOU TRIP THE FIBER-OPTIC LIGHT FANTASTIC...
BRING THIS DARK CITY TO ITS KNEES.
HAHAHAHAHA
HAHAHAHAHA

The Joker and Scarecrow have kidnapped the mayor. The Riddler is back, set on revenge. With Batman exhausted, Robin must play detective. The Firefly is trying to burn Gotham to the ground. He'd like to fry Batman at the same time. And still just watching...is Bane...
KNIGHTFALL
6
DC
DETECTIVE COMICS 661 by Dixon, Nolan, and Hanna

CITY ON FIRE
NO... PLEASE...
IT'S TIME, MR. MAYOR. YOU KNOW WHAT YOU HAVE TO DO.
NO! GET AWAY FROM ME WITH THAT THING!
CHUCK DIXON writer • GRAHAM NOLAN penciller • SCOTT HANNA inker
ADRIENNE ROY colorist • JOHN COSTANZA letterer • SCOTT PETERSON and DENNIS O'NEIL editors
• BATMAN created by BOB KANE •

TIME TO MAKE A FEW MORE CALLS, KROL...
WE WANT TO REACH OUT AND CRUSH SOMEONE.
WHO SHOULD WE HAVE HIM CALL, JOKER?
LET'S SEE. WE'VE HAD HIM CALL THE GOVERNOR AND CANCEL HIS REQUEST FOR GUARD UNITS. HE CALLED THE NEWSPAPERS AND BLAMED GORDON FOR THE SLOW RESPONSE TO THE ARKHAM BREAKOUT.
WE COULD CALL THE AIRPORT AGAIN AND HAVE THEM PAGE SEYMOUR BUTTS.
GET SERIOUS, JOKER.
OUR PLANS CALL FOR UTTER CHAOS. THINK OF SOMETHING TO MAKE THINGS HOTTER IN THE CITY.
HOTTER, EH? WHAT IF YOU CALL THE PRESIDENT OF THE FIREFIGHTERS UNION AND TOLD HIM THAT YOU WERE THINKING OF CUTTING THE ROLLS?
NOW? THEY'D STRIKE FOR CERTAIN. I WON'T DO IT.
I WON'T!
SHOWING SOME SPINE, EH?
YOU'VE FORGOTTEN WHAT ABJECT TERROR FEELS LIKE?

ALL RIGHT.
I'LL CALL.
THIS WILL BE ONE HOT NUMBER.
"HE CALLS HIMSELF THE FIREFLY. HIS REAL NAME IS GARFIELD LYNNS."
"IT'S BEEN SO LONG SINCE THEY LOCKED HIM AWAY IN ARKHAM THAT I ALMOST FORGOT HIM."
"ALMOST."
3

"HE USED TO WORK IN THE MOVIES, AN EXPERT IN PYROTECHNICS."
"HIS OCCUPATION HID HIS REAL OBSESSION."
"PYROMANIA."
"BEING HOLLYWOOD'S MASTER OF EXPLOSION AND FIRE EFFECTS WASN'T ENOUGH FOR HIM."
SO BEAUTIFUL...
YOU DANCE SO GRACEFULLY... SO LOVELY...
"HE TURNED TO ARSON FOR PROFIT."
YES... YES...
"AND THEN ARSON FOR PLEASURE."
YES! YES!
DANCE!
4

WELL, IF IT IS HIM THAT SET FIRE TO ELMO'S PIER, THEN WOULDN'T HE BE GONE BY NOW?
YOU DON'T UNDERSTAND HOW THIS MANIA WORKS, ROBIN.
IT'S NOT ENOUGH TO SET THE FIRE. HE HAS TO WATCH IT BURN. HE GETS A SICK THRILL OUT OF WATCHING IT BURN.
IT'S OUT OF HIS CONTROL. NOTHING CAN MAKE HIM TEAR HIMSELF AWAY FROM THE FLAMES.
SHOULDN'T WE WAIT UNTIL THE FIRE DEPARTMENT GETS HERE, BATMAN?
NO TIME FOR THAT. THEY'RE ALREADY OVERWHELMED. EVERY CITY SERVICE IS.
IT'S UP TO ME.
I'M TAKING THIS ONE ALONE.
YOU MEAN US.
DOGS
RESTROOMS
I DON'T LIKE THIS.
YOU DON'T HAVE TO. YOU BARELY ESCAPED KILLER CROC AND THAT MONSTER BANE. YOUR LUCK CAN'T HOLD FOREVER.
AND YOURS CAN?
5

STAY WITH THE CAR.
THE PIER BECOMES A BLAST FURNACE.
A BLISTERING WIND BEGINS TO SWIRL.
I LEAP INTO A FIRESTORM.
WELCOME TO MY INFERNO, BATMAN. ISN'T IT LOVELY?
GIVE IT UP, LYNNS. THERE'S NO WAY DOWN FROM HERE UNLESS IT'S WITH ME.
VROOOOSH
STILL THE ARROGANT ONE, EH?
WELL, YOU'RE NOT TAKING ME AS EASILY AS YOU DID BEFORE.
6

AND I'LL FIND MY OWN WAY DOWN, THANK YOU!
AHA HA HA HA HA HA!
THE WINGS ARE NEW. THE HOT THERMALS LIFT HIM.
WHOA!
A KILLING HEAT. SMOKE FILLS MY LUNGS.
CAN'T KEEP MY GRIP, LOSING IT.
HA HA HA HA HA HA HA
BATMAN! THE LINE!
SO WEAK.
HOPE I CAN MAKE THE REACH.
STOP WHINING AND DO IT.
TOO MANY LONG DAYS AND NIGHTS.
CAN'T LET THE BOY SEE HOW WASTED I AM.
7

I HATE TO SAY WHAT YOU LOOK LIKE.
I CAN MAKE IT. I DON'T NEED HELP.
YOU NEED SOMETHING. YOU'RE PUSHING TOO HARD.

I HAVE TO PUSH HARD. GOTHAM IS GOING TO HELL AT THE HANDS OF AN ARMY OF MANIACS LED BY BANE.
LET GORDON AND THE COPS TAKE CARE OF A FEW OF THEM.
THEY CAN'T. THEY DON'T KNO THE NATURE OF THESE BEASTS NOT THE WAY THAT I DO

GOD HELP ME.
I KNOW THEM.

BUT YOU CAN'T JUST THROW YOURSELF AFTER THEM. THERE'S SOMETHING TO BE SAID FOR USING OUR BRAINS, RIGHT?
NO TIME. NO TIME. WE HAVE TO REACT WHENEVER THEY SURFACE.
THAT'S NOT WHAT YOU TAUGHT ME.

ALL RIGHT.
FIREFLY IS YOURS. DO THE FOOTWORK. DIG INTO THE FILES BACK AT THE CAVE AND TRY TO GET A TWENTY ON HIM.

WHILE THERE'S STILL A CITY LEFT.
8

LOOK, IF I HELP YOU, THEN I'M AN ACCOMPLICE.
A MAN OF PRINCIPLES. ARE YOU SURE YOU'RE A LAWYER?

LET ME PLUG HIM, SOCKO. WAAAAUGH!
CALM DOWN, DUCKMAN. LOOK, YOU AGREE TO HELP US FIND SCARFACE OR MY FOWL PAL HERE IS GOING TO DRILL YOU.

I CAN'T CONTROL HIM. HE'S A WILD DUCK, COUNSELOR.
JUST TELL US WHERE TO FIND SCARFACE AND WE'RE GONE.

I'M NOT SURE WHERE HE'D BE. I GUESS HE'D BE HELD IN THE EVIDENCE ROOM OF THE PRECINCT WHERE THE VEN-TRILOQUIST WAS ARRESTED.
BUT YOU'D NEED A COP AND THE LEGIT PAPERWORK TO GET THE PROPERTY ROOM TO RELEASE HIM.

AND YOU COULD HELP US GET AHOLD OF SOME PAPERWORK, RIGHT?
SH-SURE. BUT YOU'LL STILL NEED A POLICEMAN TO GET IT RELEASED.

A CINCH, HUH, OFFICER O'HARA?
OH, IT 'TIS, IT 'TIS, ME SON. I'M YER MAN, I AM.
POLICE
9

SEVERAL CALLS FROM DR. KINSOLVING WHILE YOU WERE "OUT," MASTER BRUCE.
AND YOU TOLD HER...?
ONLY THAT YOU WERE FAR TOO BUSY DRIVING YOURSELF TO EXHAUSTION BY GALIVANTING ABOUT THE STREETS IN A MASK AND BOOTS TO SPEAK TO HER.

I'M IN NO CONDITION FOR HUMOR, ALFRED.
EXCUSE ME FOR SAYING SO, BUT YOU ARE IN NO CONDITION FOR MUCH OF ANYTHING.
A HOT SHOWER AND BREAKFAST IS ALL I NEED.

IN ADDITION TO SIXTEEN HOURS' SLEEP, A THREE-MONTH VACATION, A BLOOD TRANSFUSION AND A FULL PSYCHIATRIC EXAMINATION.
TOO MUCH NOISE. I CAN'T HEAR YOU, ALFRED.

NOT THAT YOU EVER COULD.
AND WHERE IS MASTER TIM THIS FINE AFTERNOON?

RUNNING DOWN SOME BACKGROUND FOR ME.
10

GARFIELD LYNNS. HE'S BEEN LOCKED UP SO LONG THAT THERE'S NOT MUCH IN THE NETWORKS ABOUT HIM.
NOTHING AT DMV. NO CREDIT HISTORY. NOTHING FROM ARKHAM SINCE THE PLACE GOT NUKED. HE'S A BLANK SLATE EXCEPT FOR HIS POLICE FILE.
ARREST RECORD GOES BACK TO JUVIE. MULTIPLE COUNTS OF ARSON AND RECKLESS ENDANGERMENT. EVEN AN ATTEMPTED HOMICIDE.
NO NAMES LISTED FOR HIS PARENTS.
HM. LEGAL GUARDIAN, ST. EVANGELINA HOME FOR BOYS.
LYNNS IS AN ORPHAN. IT'S BEEN A LONG TIME BUT MAYBE SOMEONE THERE REMEMBERS HIM.
ANYTHING WOULD BE MORE HELPFUL THAN THE LITTLE BIT THAT I'VE GOT.
ALL I HAVE TO DO NOW IS FIGURE WHAT EXCUSE I'M GOING TO USE TO GET OUT OF THE HOUSE TONIGHT.
I CAN TELL DAD THAT I'M SPENDING THE NIGHT AT IVES' HOUSE.
I TOLD IVES THAT I'M GOING INTO TOWN TO SEE ARIANA.
THE LYING IS THE ONLY PART OF THIS JOB THAT I HATE.
11

THAT AND THE LONG HOURS.
BUT HOW CAN I COMPLAIN WHEN BATMAN IS PUSHING HIMSELF SO HARD?
NO LUCK.
THIS PLACE HAS BEEN CLOSED FOR AGES.
A DEAD END.
BUT I HAVE TO COME BACK WITH SOME-THING.
QUIET HERE.
MAYBE THE ONLY PEACEFUL PLACE IN ALL OF GOTHAM.
IS SOMEONE THERE?
UH?
UH... I'M SORRY IF I BOTHERED YOU.
NO BOTHER. I'M JUST NOT USED TO SHARING THE COURT-YARD WITH ANYONE.

YOU SOUND YOUNG.
THERE HAVEN'T BEEN ANY YOUNG MEN HERE SINCE THEY CLOSED THE ORPHANAGE TWENTY YEARS AGO.
THERE'S JUST MYSELF AND A FEW OF THE OTHER OLD SISTERS.

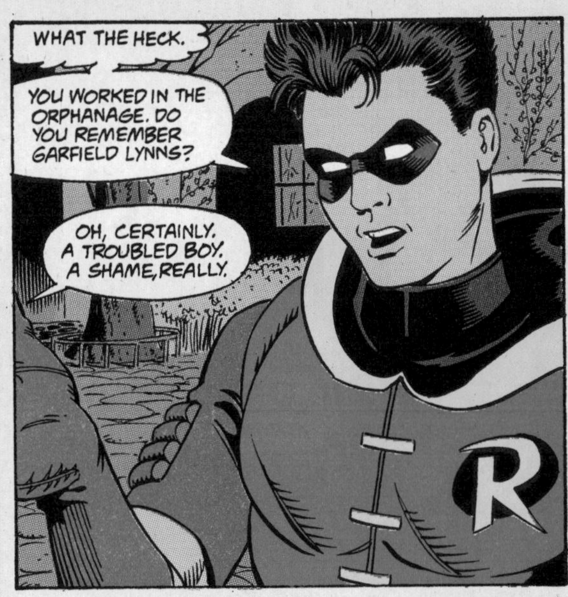
WHAT THE HECK.
YOU WORKED IN THE ORPHANAGE. DO YOU REMEMBER GARFIELD LYNNS?
OH, CERTAINLY. A TROUBLED BOY. A SHAME, REALLY.

WE DID ALL THAT WE COULD FOR HIM BUT...
AND HIS SISTER WAS SUCH A WONDERFUL GIRL. A JOY.
A SISTER?

YES. HER NAME WAS... AMANDA. YOUNGER THAN GARFIELD. I DON'T RECALL WHERE SHE WENT AFTER SHE LEFT HERE.
SHE COULD STILL BE IN GOTHAM CITY.

SHE SHOULD BE EASY TO FIND THROUGH CREDIT BUREAUS OR VOTER REGISTRATION.
SISTER, DO YOU THINK--

WOW.
SHE COULD GIVE BATMAN SOME LESSONS IN DRAMATIC EXITS.
13

--AND POWER HAS YET TO BE RESTORED TO LYNTOWN, EASTOWN OR SHELDON PARK.

HOT TOWN TONIGHT?

WE NOW JOIN THE LINK RAMBEAU SHOW, ALREADY IN PROGRESS.

LINK Rambeau

LET ME GET THIS STRAIGHT, DOC. YOU'RE SAYING THAT IT'S OUR FAULT THAT THESE SQUIRRELS ARE TEARING OUR CITY APART?

ABSOLUTELY. OUR ENTIRE CULTURE IS ABERRANT.

THESE DANGEROUS INDIVIDUALS NOW CAUSING SUCH AN INCONVENIENCE ARE MERELY SYMPTOMS OF THAT ABERRATION.

LINK Rambeau

"AN INCONVENIENCE." WE HAVE A BODY COUNT RIVALING SARAJEVO. PARTS OF THE CITY BURN OUT OF CONTROL. LAWLESSNESS AND CHAOS ARE THE ORDER OF THE DAY.

AND WE ENCOURAGE THIS, RIGHT?

IT'S ALL RIGHT HERE IN "I'M SANE AND SO ARE YOU"!
ALL OF US MUST SHARE THE BLAME.
I'M SANE AND SO ARE YOU

YOU HEARD IT HERE FIRST, FOLKS...
IF SOME PSYCHO CUTS YOUR HEART OUT BECAUSE HIS SALISBURY STEAK TOLD HIM TO...

...IT'S ALL YOUR FAULT.
AIN'T THERE A GAME ON?
IT'S BLACKED OUT.
JEEZE. I NEVER BEEN SO BORED IN MY LIFE.
STAN'S RIGHT, RIDDLER. THIS IS A STONE DRAG. WHEN WE GONNA MAKE OUR MOVE?

I TOLD YOU DUNCES THAT THESE THINGS TAKE PLANNING. YOU HAVE TO CROSS YOUR TEES AND DOT YOUR EYES. EVERYTHING IN ITS PLACE AND A PLACE FOR EVERY-THING.

WHAT'S THE HOLD-UP? WE ALREADY GOT THE TALENT, THE GETAWAY CARS AND THE BUILDING PLANS.
IT'S JUST A JOB TO YOU, ISN'T IT, BONEY?

TO ME IT'S THE HIGHEST FORM OF ART.
IT SHOULDN'T BE WORKMANLIKE DRUDGERY. CRIME DEMANDS A CERTAIN AMOUNT OF FLAIR. WIT.
GLUE

IF BREAKING THE LAW CAN'T BE FUN, THEN WHAT GOOD IS IT?
PolicE HeADQuarteRs
GoTham CenTral
URGenT
15

YOU HAVE THE RIGHT TO REMAIN SILENT...
WHAT TIME IS IT?
ANYTHING YOU SAY MAY BE USED AGAINST YOU IN A COURT OF LAW.
WHAT TIME IS IT?
WHAT TIME IS IT?
WHAT TIME IS IT?
NAP TIME!
UNNH!
THAT WAS UNCALLED FOR, BULLOCK.
PISTOL-WHIPPING IS NOT STANDARD PROCEDURE.
WELL, YOU WEREN'T HELPIN' MUCH READING HIM HIS MIRANDAS, KITCH.
LIKE WE GOT TIME FOR YOUR PRECIOUS PROCEDURES WITH THESE ANIMALS RUNNING ALL OVER TOWN.
16

HENDRICKS, WHAT ARE YOU DOING?
JUST CATCHIN' UP WITH YESTERDAY'S MAIL, SARGE.
YOU COULD HAVE LENT A HAND OVER THERE.
EVERYBODY GRAB A UNIT AND GET OVER TO CASTLELAND PARK. WE GOT THREE PERPS WITH ROCKET LAUNCHERS SHOOTING THE PLACE UP AND WE'RE CATCHING IT.
SINCE WHEN ARE WE TACTICAL?
SINCE YOU ALL VOLUNTEERED.
LT. NEWTON
HENDRICKS, WHAT ARE YOU DOING?
JUST CATCHING UP WITH--
WELL, DROP IT AND GRAB A SHOTGUN. WE NEED EVERYBODY ON THIS.
GOTHAM POLICE DEPT. CENTRAL DIVISION
YEAH, I GUESS THIS CAN WAIT, HUH?
POLICE HEADQUARTERS
GOTHAM CENTRAL
URGENT
17

AMANDA LYNNS?
I'M OFFICER MONTOYA. THIS IS OFFICER CARBERRY. MAY WE COME IN?
WELL, IT'S AMANDA KELSO NOW.
WE WERE TOLD THAT YOU—
I KNOW WHY YOU'RE HERE. BUT I HAVEN'T SEEN GARFIELD. HE DIDN'T COME HERE WHEN HE ESCAPED.
THAT WOULD HAVE BEEN MY FIRST QUESTION. HE'S BURNT DOWN ELMO'S PIER. WE WERE WONDERING IF YOU KNEW WHY.
GOD...
WE WERE ORPHANS... PEOPLE WOULD COME TO SEE US, TO ADOPT US...
THEY'D TALK ABOUT THE PLACES THEY'D TAKE US WHEN WE BECAME THEIR CHILDREN. BUT WHEN THEY LOOKED INTO GARFIELD'S PAST...
...THEY'D GO AWAY. WE'D NEVER SEE THEM AGAIN.
WHAT OTHER PLACES DID THEY SAY THEY WOULD TAKE YOU?
OH, YOU KNOW... THE KIND OF PLACES KIDS LOVE TO GO...
THE MAJESTIC THEATER, THE BOWLING ALLEY IN LYNNWOOD... THE ZOO... GARFIELD HATED THEM FOR THEIR PROMISES...
AMAZING WHAT AN ANONYMOUS PHONE CALL CAN DO.
18

ONE OF THE LESSER MANIACS.
THE CAVALIER FANCIES HIMSELF SOME KIND OF EXPERT IN THE FENCING ARTS.
BUT I DON'T HAVE TIME FOR ART.
YOU BROGE BY DOSE, YOU CAD!
BATMAN?
JUST A SECOND... ROBIN.
I JUST BRING HIM DOWN.
A LIGHTWEIGHT THUG. BUT IT TAKES EVERYTHING I'VE GOT TO TAKE HIM.
BATMAN? CAN YOU READ ME, BATMAN?
I'M HERE, ROBIN. GO AHEAD.
19

I'VE GOT A LIST OF POSSIBLE TARGETS FOR THE FIREFLY.
GIVE THEM TO ME.
THE GOTHAM PARK ZOO. THE ORPHEUM MAJESTIC THEATER IN GLENDALE AND THE LYNNWOOD LANES BOWLING ALLEY.
I'M CLOSEST TO THE LYNNWOOD. I'LL CHECK THAT FIRST.
GOOD WORK, ROBIN.
YOU CAN TELL ME LATER WHERE YOU GOT THAT LIST.
THE ROAR AND CRACKLE, THE GLORIOUS LIGHT. IT IS ALL SO... SOOTHING.
THE BOWLING ALLEY IS A PARKING LOT NOW.
20

THE MAJESTIC IS NEXT. IT HASN'T BEEN A THEATER FOR YEARS. THESE DAYS IT'S A FURNITURE WAREHOUSE.
BURN... BURN... BURN!
MAJESTIC
FURNITURE
IT DOESN'T SEEM TO MATTER TO LYNNS.
YOU'RE GETTING TO BE A PEST, BATMAN.
I'M NOT ONE OF THOSE ARKHAM INMATES WHO OBSESSED OVER YOU DAY AND NIGHT.
IN FACT, I'LL GET ALONG QUITE NICELY WITHOUT YOUR INTERFERENCE.
BUT IF YOU SPOIL MY FUN ONE MORE TIME I MAY BE FORCED TO CHANGE MY MIND ABOUT THAT!
YOU REALLY ARE A WET BLANKET, BATTY.
21

ROOF IS AS HOT AS A SKILLET UNDER MY FEET.
THE SAME HEAT WILL CARRY HIM AWAY AGAIN.
DON'T THINK. JUST ACT.
NO!
YOU'LL KILL US BOTH!
THE INFERNO COMES UP TO MEET US, EMBRACE US.
LOOKS LIKE MY WORLD WILL END IN FIRE.

Batman and Firefly burn up the night.
Azrael tests himself in action.
Scarecrow and Joker torment Mayor Krol.
Poison Ivy kidnaps Wayne Foundation's Lucius Fox,
to transform him into her vile Deadfellow slave!
Elsewhere, Bruce and Shondra attend a dinner together...
Under Bane's "paternal" eye...
7
KNIGHTFALL
DC

BATMAN 495 by
Moench, Aparo and Wiacek.

STRANGE DEAD FELLOWS

PULLING US BOTH DOWN -- STRAIGHT INTO HELL.

NO! YOU'LL KILL US BURN US ALIVE!

ANOTHER MADMAN HATCHED FROM SHATTERED ARKHAM -- THE FIREFLY -- PYROMANIAC...

HE DESERVES IT -- MAYBE WE BOTH DO...

...BUT GOT TO LET HIM GO...

THIS END UP

BATMAN CREATED BY BOB KANE

DOUG MOENCH WRITER
JIM APARO PENCILLER
BOB WIACEK INKER
ADRIENNE ROY COLORIST
RICHARD STARKINGS LETTERER
JORDAN B. GORFINKEL ASST. EDITOR
DENNIS O'NEIL EDITOR

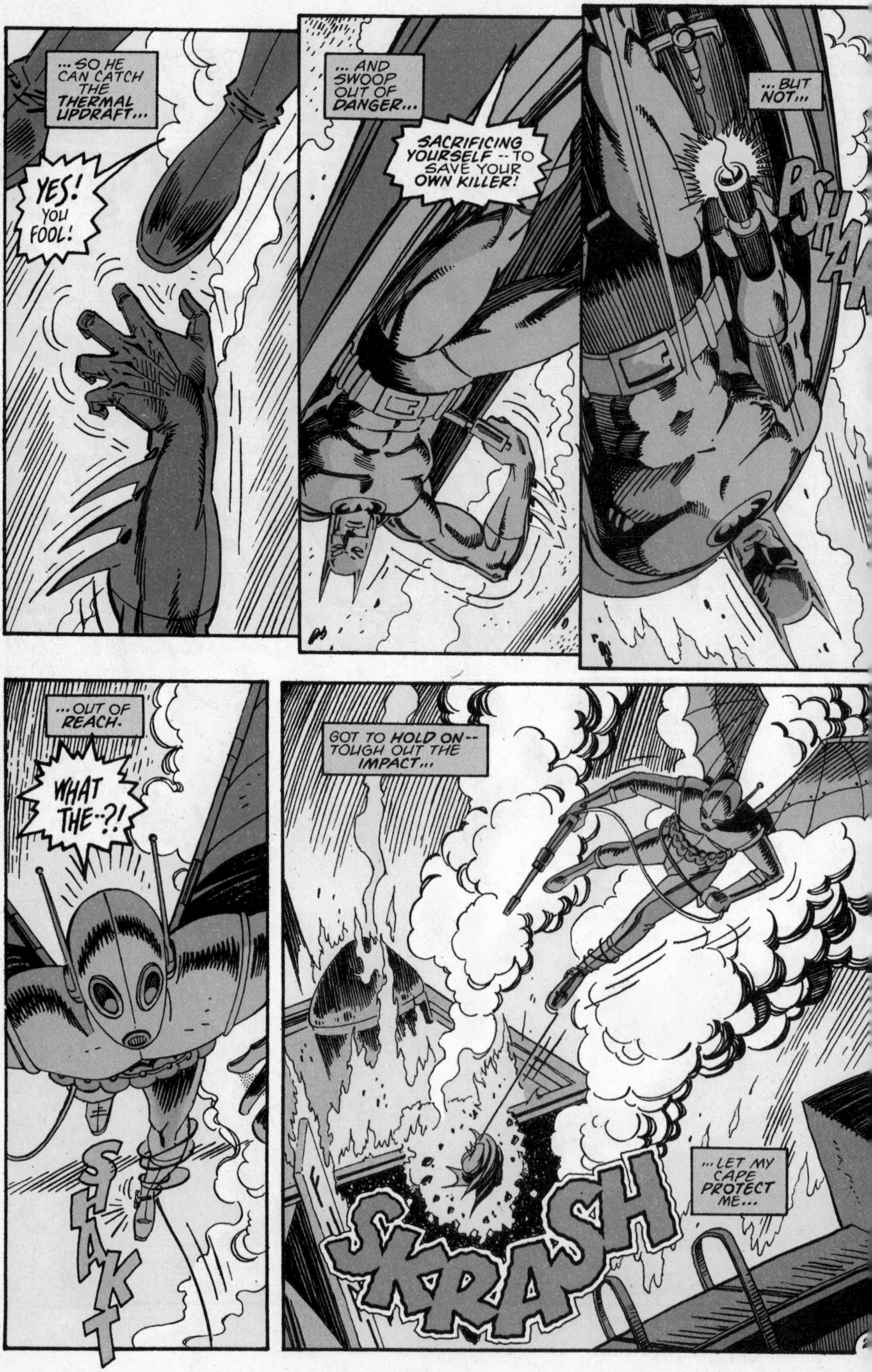

...SO HE CAN CATCH THE THERMAL UPDRAFT...
YES! YOU FOOL!

...AND SWOOP OUT OF DANGER...
SACRIFICING YOURSELF -- TO SAVE YOUR OWN KILLER!

...BUT NOT...
PSHAK

...OUT OF REACH.
WHAT THE--?!

GOT TO HOLD ON-- TOUGH OUT THE IMPACT...
...LET MY CAPE PROTECT ME...
SKRASH

MOST PERSISTENT, AREN'T YOU, BATMAN?
SHROOM

BUT THEN... SO AM I!
SPAPT

ONE CHANCE LEFT...

FWP
WP
WP
BTANKT
UNFF!
FIRE ESCAPE.
3

BUT ONE WAY OR ANOTHER... STILL BURNING OUT.
THIS TIME... COULDN'T EVEN STOP A MINOR ONE LIKE THE FIREFLY...
AND IF THIS KEEPS UP... THE WHOLE CITY GOES TO HELL.

STILL FEEL LIKE HELL, EVEN AFTER WEEKS OF THOUSAND-PUSHUP DAYS...

BUT THE PROBLEM, OF COURSE, IS HARDLY PHYSICAL.
AFTER THAT DISASTROUS ENCOUNTER WITH KILLER CROC, I'VE GOT TO REDEEM MYSELF... PROVE MYSELF WORTHY...
CHAKT

...EVEN IF ONLY WORTHY OF THIS IMITATION COSTUME, NEITHER AZRAEL NOR BATMAN.
AND SINCE CALISTHENICS PROVE NOTHING, IT'S TIME TO TEST MYSELF BY "FIRE" -- FOR REAL AND WITHOUT ROBIN.

--CHARITY FUNCTION TONIGHT, SIR, AND ALTHOUGH I'M LOATH TO URGE ATTENDANCE IN YOUR PRESENT CONDITION--
--IT SHOULD PERHAPS BE POINTED OUT THAT THE PUBLIC IS WELL AWARE OF THE BATMAN BEING RUN RAGGED OF LATE...
...AND WERE BRUCE WAYNE TO CONCURRENTLY DROP FROM SIGHT, FAILING TO APPEAR AT A WAYNE FOUNDATION DINNER, PLANNED MONTHS IN AD--
ENOUGH, ALFRED...
AT THIS POINT, I COULDN'T CARE LESS ABOUT SUCH CONSIDERATIONS ... BUT I WILL ATTEND.
YOU WILL, SIR?!
WITH SO MANY MANIACS STILL LOOSE IN GOTHAM... TONIGHT'S GATHERING MAKES FOR A RIPE TARGET.
IN ONE MASK OR THE OTHER...
...I HAVE TO BE THERE.
WHATEVER GETS YOU THROUGH THE DAY, SIR, AND TO THAT DINNER TONIGHT.
I SHALL AWAKEN YOU AS LATE AS POSSIBLE.
5

AWAKEN, MY SWEET DEAD-FELLOW... AND JOIN THE OTHERS...

THIS IS A MOST IMPORTANT NIGHT...

...AND I WANT YOU TO PREPARE FOR MY RETURN.

BIRD TO BANE: I'VE BEEN FOLLOWING ANOTHER OF THE ARKHAM ESCAPEES -- AND I'VE GOT A FEELING SOMETHING'S ABOUT TO GO DOWN...

YOU WANNA SEE IT UNFOLD, BETTER GET DOWN HERE TO THE CIVIC CENTER NOW...
GOTHAM CIVIC CENT

COULD BE MORE FUN, IF THE BATMAN SHOWS.
IF THERE'S TROUBLE, BIRD, HE'LL BE THERE -- AND SO WILL I.

YOU KNOW, BEFORE ARKHAM, I GOT L-WOPPED BIG TIME.
"EL WOPPED?"
L-WOPPED.
LIFE -- WITHOUT POSSIBILITY OF PAROLE.
POTATO CHIPS

Ahah -- THAT IS BIG TIME, SCARECROW -- THE BIGGEST TIME YOU CAN DO.
ALL IN ALL, I'D SAY BEING CRAZY IS BETTER.

BUT, BEST OF ALL IS THIS, SCARECROW -- BEING BUSTED OUT -- WITHOUT GETTING BETTER!
HA HAHAHA HA
INDEED, JOKER -- ANY TIME YOU CAN BE CURED OF CONFINEMENT, IT'S BETTER.

BUT NOW... IT'S PHONE-TIME AGAIN!
FEAR-GAS TIME TOO!
SKSH
YOU'RE GOING TO SEND EVERY COP IN THIS CITY ON A WILD GOOSE CHASE, MAYOR KROL -- TO GET THEIR GOOSES COOKED!
HAHA
7

--ACTUALLY LOOK *FEVERED*, BRUCE, AND IF YOU CONTINUE CANCELING OUR *APPOINTMENTS* --
PLEASE, SHONDRA, I'M FEELING *FINE*.
THE ONLY MEDICINE I NEED TONIGHT IS YOUR PRESENCE AT MY TABLE...

THE ONE NEAR THE ENTRANCE -- WITH THE BLACK WOMAN -- IT'S *HIM*.

YEAH, THAT'S *BRUCE WAYNE*, ALL RIGHT, *HOST* OF THIS BASH... BUT HOW HE FIGURES INTO WHAT'S GOING DOWN --
IT'S *NOT* "BRUCE WAYNE..."

IT'S *HIM*.

YOU... YOU MEAN... THE *BATMAN*? BUT... HOW CAN YOU BE SO *SURE*, BANE?

I KNOW HIM *INTIMATELY* NOW, BIRD...

"...HE CANNOT *HIDE* FROM ME SIMPLY BY *REMOVING HIS MASK!*"

NO POLICE PROTECTION *ANYWHERE* -- SOME THING'S *WRONG*... *SERIOUSLY* WRONG.

BRUCE?

IS... IS ANYTHING *WRONG*?

NOT AT *ALL*, SHONDRA -- I'M SURE THE EVENING WILL BE *WONDERFUL*.

BRACE YOURSELF FOR ONE LOUSY NIGHT, COMMISH -- MAYOR KROL'S BEEN KIDNAPPED!
BASH
HOW--?
BEATS ME, BUT KROL HIMSELF SOMEHOW GOT TO A 'PHONE...
...LONG ENOUGH TO GIVE THE LOCATION BEFORE HE WAS CUT OFF BY THE KIDNA--
WHERE--?
THE ABANDONED AMUSEMENT PARK IN SEAGATE...
EVERY COP IN THE CITY'S ALREADY ON THE WAY...
THEN LET'S ROLL, BULLOCK -- BEFORE WE'RE THE EXCEPTION.
--EXCEPTIONAL GENEROSITY OF THE WAYNE FOUNDATION IN FUNDING THE FREE CLINIC WORK BEING DONE BY DOCTOR SHONDRA KINSOLVING UNDER MY SUPERVISION...
THIS IS HARDLY THE PLACE TO BRING IT UP, BUT YOU'VE BEEN UNAVAILABLE FOR SO LONG THAT I --
GO AHEAD, LUCIUS...
9

WELL, IT'S JUST THAT I KNOW YOU'RE NOT THE FUZZY DOLT YOU PRETEND TO BE IN BUSINESS MATTERS, BUT LATELY YOU'VE ACTUALLY BEGUN NEGLECTING WAYNE-CORP'S AFFAIRS--
STARTING TO FEEL... DIZZY...

S-SOMETHING'S WRONG... CLOYING NARCOTIC SCENT...
--TO THE POINT THAT I CAN'T STOP THE PIN-WHEELS SPINNING OUT OF CONTROL IN YOUR EYES STRANGLING ME AND... AND...

G-GOT TO GET... BREATHING FILTERS... BEFORE... LOSE CONTROL...

--AND SO I'D LIKE TO PRESENT OUR GUEST OF ON THE PLATFORM OF DAZZLING SPARKS SHOOTING FROM ALL THE BRIGHTS OF ADDLED OWLS SWOOPING MICE AND... BUT...
YOU SEEM TO BE HAVING TROUBLE WITH YOUR TONGUE, DOCTOR TOMPKINS.
I'LL TAKE OVER FROM HERE...

TA-DAA!
INSERTED THE NOSE-FILTERS JUST IN TIME... HEAD STARTING TO CLEAR...
POISON IVY!
20

THE PLANTS -- SOME NIGHTSHADE VARIANT... BLOOMING RIGHT IN HE MIDDLE OF THE DINNER, RELEASING THEIR SPORES... NO OUBT GENETICALLY LTERED BY IVY'S NOWLEDGE OF BOTANY...
WE'RE MOVING THE PARTY, GENTLEMEN, TO A NEW LOCALE...

...WHICH ALSO HAPPENS TO BE THE NEW BENEFICIARY OF YOUR CHARITABLE LARGESSE.
LUCKY US, THE POLICE SEEM TO BE OCCUPIED ELSEWHERE, BUT IF YOU WILL KINDLY FILE OUT THE REAR EXIT ANYWAY -- GENTLEMEN ONLY -- YOU WILL FIND A TRUCK WAITING OUTSIDE.

BEST TO PLAY ALONG... PRETEND I'M ONE OF IVY'S ZOMBIES... UNTIL I CAN LEARN IF SHE'S ALREADY CAPTURED OTHER VICTIMS...
AS FOR YOU LADIES... THE DIURNAL SPORE CYCLE WILL END IN SEVERAL HOURS...

UNTIL THEN, ENJOY SOME GROUP NAP THERAPY...

...COURTESY OF POISON IVY'S NON-PATENTED NIGHTSHADE HYBRIDS, BELOVED SCENT OF ZOMBIES EVERYWHERE.
11

ALL ABOARD, GENTLEMEN!
NEXT STOP -- NEO EDEN.
NEO EDEN
PLANTS & FLOWERS FOR ALL OCCASIONS
LOOKS LIKE SHE PUT 'EM ALL INTO SOME KIND OF TRANCE, BANE...
OBVIOUSLY, BIRD... BUT HE IS MERELY FEIGNING.
Huh? HOW CAN YOU POSSIBLY KNOW THA -- ?
FOLLOW THEM -- AND GIVE ME RADIO UPDATES.
ABANDON HOPE, ALL YE WHO ENTER HERE -- HOPE FOR YOUR MISERABLE MAYOR'S LIFE, THAT IS!
HAHAHAHA
FUN H SE
THAT'S THE JOKER, ALL RIGHT -- WHAT DO WE DO?
WAIT FOR COMMISSIONER GORDON -- HE GETS PAID TO DECIDE THINGS LIKE THAT!
12

SO I HEAR ON THE WAY OVER HERE THAT SOME MAGOOK WITH BIG BRASS ONES JUST SNATCHED THE MAYOR, S'POSEDLY GOT 'IM STASHED IN THE OLD SEAGATE AMUSE-MENT PAR--
WHY DO I CARE ABOUT THE MAYOR, MIKEY, WHEN YOU'RE MAKING ME NERVOUS AGAIN? JUST JIMMY THAT LOCK, WILLYA, BEFORE--
Uh Oh
THE BATMAN?
SURE FEELS LIKE...
HEY -- YOU'RE NOT THE BATMAN!
NO. I'M NOT.
SHUMP
KRUNCH
THRAKK
YOUR BAD LUCK.
13

WELCOME TO NEO EDEN, GENTLEMEN, ONE OF MY HOMES AWAY FROM HOME -- EVEN BEFORE I LAST ENJOYED ARKHAM'S HOSPITALITY -- AND CONCEALED FROM THE OUTSIDE WORLD BY MY OWN BOTANIC TWIST ON THE KUDZU VINE...
NOW, SINCE THERE'S NO REAL RUSH IN FLEECING YOU, IF YOU'LL ALL LINE UP LIKE THE DEAR SWEET WEALTHY GENTLEMEN YOU ARE...
...I JUST MIGHT FEEL INCLINED TO ADMINISTER YOUR REWARD...
CAN'T AFFORD TO PLAY POSSUM ANY LONGER.
IVY'S LIKE TYPHOID MARY -- A WALKING PLAGUE, HER SYSTEM FULL OF TOXINS TO WHICH ONLY SHE'S IMMUNE...
...AND WHETHER SHE'S AFTER THEIR MONEY, THEIR POWER, OR BOTH...
...IF SHE KISSES THEM, SHE'LL KILL THEM.
14

HOLD STILL, MY DEAR, SWEET, VEGETATING SUGAR-DADDY...
HERE...
IT...
C--!?!
FWIK
YOU... STILL THE DARK ANGEL, IMMUNE TO MY ALLURE, EVER TEMPTED, NEVER SUCCUMBING.
AND YOU'VE COME TO SAVE THEM...
HOW NOBLE, BATMAN... HOW WRETCHEDLY, DISGUSTINGLY NOBLE.
FORTUNATELY, HOWEVER, YOU'RE TOO LATE TO SAVE CERTAIN OTHERS... WHO ARE ALREADY IN A MORE ADVANCED STATE OF OBSESSION...
HARDLY GOTHAM'S WEALTHIEST AND MOST INFLUENTIAL MEN, BUT DEFINITELY THE CREAM OF THE CROP IN PHYSICAL ASSETS... AND A PREVIEW OF WHAT AWAITS MY NEWEST ZOMBIES...
DEAD-FELLOWS--!
SNAP
BEAT HIM UNTIL HE BEGS FOR MY KISS--
15

NYAHRR
FIVE OF THEM...
...ALL INFECTED.
CAN'T RISK OPEN WOUNDS.
SWUT
WUKT
ON ME.

AND I CAN'T WASTE ANY TIME...

...NOT WITH IVY'S BLOODY MOUTH STILL BREATHING...
KISSSSS...

...STILL THREATENING TO POISON HER NEW PUPPETS...
LUCIUS!
16

SWUMP
STILL IN BAD SHAPE -- EXHAUSTION KICKING IN FROM THE FIRST MOVE NOW...
FWAK
WAK
ENERGY DEPLETING ALMOST IMMEDIATELY...
TUD
DRAINED BEFORE I START...
HWOK
CHUT
17

SWOK

...TO HELL WITH ALL WEAKNESS...

FULL SPEED...

...AHEAD.
CHUNT

THE SHOCK... ALL THE WAY UP MY SPINE... EXPLODING IN MY SKULL.
DIZZY... DIM...
FIGHT IT.
WUMP

BIRD TO BANE: LOOKS LIKE HE'S GONNA DO IT AGAIN... EVEN IF HE ENDS LIKE A RAG DOLL.
HE'S STILL STANDING...

...BUT HE SURE WANTS TO FALL.
PERFECT.

THEY'RE TERMINAL, AREN'T THEY?
TERMINALLY OBEDIENT... TERMINALLY IN LOVE WITH MY KISS...
THERE'S NO ANTI-DOTE...

...NO HOPE FOR THEM?
THEY WOULD HAVE GLADLY DIED DAYS AGO...
...MORE THAN SATISFIED WITH WHAT I'VE ALREADY GIVEN THEM...
19

AND DON'T YOU THINK IT'S FINALLY TIME FOR YOU, DEAR SWEET BATMAN...
...TO SURRENDER.

YOU MEAN --

-- TO A WITCH?!
FTAK
GOT TO GET LUCIUS AND THE OTHERS OUT OF HERE, AWAY FROM THE NIGHT-SHADE SPORES...
...AWAY FROM IVY.
I NEED AMBULANCES -- LOTS OF THEM.
EQUIP THE ATTENDANTS WITH GAS-MASKS...

N-NO... DON'T...PLEASE NOT AGAIN... PLEASE... DON'T... EEYAAAIEE
THAT'S KROL'S VOICE --HE'S BEING TORTURED IN THERE...
TORTURED...?

...SOUNDS MORE LIKE HE'S BEIN' MURDERED, COMMISH... AN' MAYBE WE CAN'T AFFORD TO WAIT ANY--
ALL RIGHT...
...SEND IN THE SWAT TEAM-- NOW!

MOVE IT-- RUSH 'EM!
GO, GO GO!

WHAT THE--? NOTHING BUT A TAPE-PLAYER?
SURPRISE, SURPRISE, SUCKERS!
WAIT-- UNDER THE TABLE...

LOOKS LIKE... A B--
21

YOUR BEST **PHONE CALL** BY FAR, MAYOR KROL!

HA HA HAHA

A BOFFO SMASH HIT!

UNLIKE SOME OF THE *OTHERS*, BANE, THIS JOKER PREFERS THE ***DIRECT*** APPROACH.

INDEED, ZOMBIE, AND LET US HOPE OUR PREY ENDURES ***PAST*** THE JOKER.

BUT ***WHY***, BANE? IF THE JOKER CAN TAKE BATMAN ***OUT***, WHY *NOT*?

BECAUSE HE'S ***MINE***, TROGG.

MINE TO ***CRACK***.

MINE TO ***BREAK***.

The Riddler threatens to kill a talk-show audience.
Only Robin has a chance of saving them.
The Huntress watches over a city in flames.
And Batman tries one last time to take down the Firefly.
As Gotham burns...and Bane waits...
KNIGHTFALL
8
DETECTIVE COMICS 662
by Dixon, Nolan, and Hanna
DC

BURNING QUESTIONS
WHAT'S THE DEAL HERE, GUYS? CAN'T WE TALK ABOUT THIS?
THAT'S ALL YOU DO IS TALK, RIDDLER.
AND WE'RE SICK OF IT AND SICK OF YOU!
CHUCK DIXON writer
GRAHAM NOLAN penciler
SCOTT HANNA inker
ADRIENNE ROY colorist
JOHN COSTANZA letterer
SCOTT PETERSON and DENNIS O'NEIL editors
BATMAN created by BOB KANE

BONEY! STAN! PHIL! PLEASE!
WE PLANNED THIS JOB TO A "T" AND WE'RE READY TO GO, EVERYTHING IN PLACE.
BLAM BLAM
BUT DO WE MAKE OUR MOVE? NO!
BLAM BOOM
WE GOTTA WAIT UNTIL YOU SEND OUT YOUR STUPID RIDDLES!
WELL, WE'RE PULLIN' THIS JOB TONIGHT AND IF IT HAS TO BE OVER YOUR DEAD BODY...

...THEN THAT'S THE WAY IT'S GONNA BE!
BLAM
BLAM
BLAM
BLAM
SPUDSY
Amber Ale
BEERO
NON ALCOHOLIC BREW

THAT'S IT! RUN BACK TO ARKHAM! THEY GOT A WARM BED AND A COZY STRAIT-JACKET WAITIN'!
EMERGENCY EXIT

MEBBE WE SHUNNA LET HIM GO, BONEY. THE CREEP MIGHT RAT US OUT.
IF YOU THINK HE MIGHT GO TO THE COPS AND TELL HIM FLAT-OUT WHAT WE WAS PLANNIN' THEN YOU DON'T UNDER-STAND THE RIDDLER.

HOW CAN I GET MY PUZZLES BEFORE THE MASSES? HOW CAN I REACH THEM...?

HOLD ON...

...*FOR A LIMITED TIME ONLY!*

APPLIA

ENTE

SO CALL BEFORE MIDNIGHT TONIGHT FOR YOUR HITS OF THE SEVENTIES COLLECTION.

EUREKA.

3

IS THIS HOW YOU PLAN ON SPENDING YOUR ENTIRE SUMMER VACATION?
THUP
THUP
THUP
THUP
THROP!
I'M JUST.
THUD!
WORKING OUT.
WHUD!
A LITTLE *FRUSTRATION.*
I DID ALL THE FOOTWORK ON THE FIREFLY CASE AND BATMAN'S MAKING ME SIT OUT THE BUST.
SO WHILE HE GOES FOR THE GLORY...
DENIED THE OPPORTUNITY TO CONFRONT A PSYCHOTIC ARSONIST. I CAN ONLY *IMAGINE* YOUR DISAPPOINTMENT.
...I GET TO WATCH IT ALL ON THE TUBE.
AND WHERE DID YOUR INVESTIGATIONS LEAD YOU?
THE GOTHAM PARK ZOO.
IT WAS LAST ON THE FIREFLY'S LIST.
4

GARFIELD LYNNS IS OUT TO BURN DOWN ALL OF THE PLACES HE NEVER GOT TAKEN TO AS A CHILD.
IN PSYCHOBABBLE TERMS HE'S FEEDING OFF THE RAGE OF HIS INNER CHILD, REDRESSING THE DISAPPOINTMENTS OF HIS PAST.

BUT THE FIREFLY IS NO VICTIM.
HE'S A DANGER TO HIMSELF AND EVERYONE HE COMES IN CONTACT WITH.

AND A TORTURED CHILDHOOD IS NO EXCUSE FOR BECOMING A MONSTER.
I KNOW.
5

WHAT *ARE* YOU DOING?
CHANNEL SURFING. THERE'S NOTHING ON.
HOW WOULD YOU *KNOW?* YOU DON'T WATCH ANYTHING FOR LONGER THAN THREE SECONDS.
KLIK KLIK KLIK KLIK KLIK
YOU NEVER DO THIS?

I TEND TO WATCH A PROGRAM FROM ITS *BEGINNING* UNTIL ITS *END* AND THEN I SWITCH THE SET *OFF*.
WOW, *THIS* GUY'S GETTING A LOT OF MILEAGE OUT OF THE ARKHAM BREAKOUT.

AND HE IS...
SOME PSYCHIATRIST WHO WORKED ON STAFF AT THE ASYLUM. HE'S BEEN ON ALMOST EVERY TALK SHOW PUSHING SOME POP PSYCH BOOK HE WROTE.
NOW HE'S ON CASSIE JOSIE RUDOLPHO'S SHOW.
HM.

AND YOU SAY THAT THESE MEN ARE MERELY TROUBLED CHILDREN SEARCHING FOR MEANING IN THEIR LIVES?
EXACTLY, CASSIE. IT'S JUST AS I'VE DETAILED IN MY BOOK, "I'M SANE AND SO ARE YOU."
THESE MEN ARE SOCIETY'S VICTIMS, NOT THE OTHER WAY AROUND.
I'M SANE AND SO ARE YOU

6

WELL. LET'S GIVE OUR AUDIENCE A CHANCE TO QUESTION DR. FLANDERS.
DO ANY OF YOU HAVE ANYTHING TO ASK OUR GUEST?
THE
Ca
ACTUALLY, CASSIE, I HAD A NUMBER OF QUESTIONS.
GO AHEAD, SIR. THIS IS AN OPEN FORUM.
WHAT LETTER IS NEVER FOUND IN THE ALPHABET?
WHAT DOES THE BALLPLAYER LIKE TO BE CALLED AT HOME?
I'M NOT SURE I--
OH MY GOD!
WHAT TRAVELS AROUND THE WORLD BUT NEVER LEAVES ITS CORNER?
WHY WAS THE LETTER DAMP?
LET'S GET TO THE VAN, ALFRED! THAT SHOW ORIGINATES IN GOTHAM.
BUT...
COME ON, IT AIRS LIVE!
7

THE FIRST SIGN OF DANGER IS THE ANIMALS.

THEY'RE REACTING TO A THREAT.

THEN THE GLOW OF FIRE.

THEN THAT MADDENING LAUGHTER ON THE SUMMER WIND.

IT RISES EVEN OVER THE HOWL OF THE TERRIFIED ANIMALS.
HA HA HA HA HOO HAHA!
BEAUTIFUL! BEAUTIFUL!
BY FAR MY BEST EFFORT!
FLAMABLE

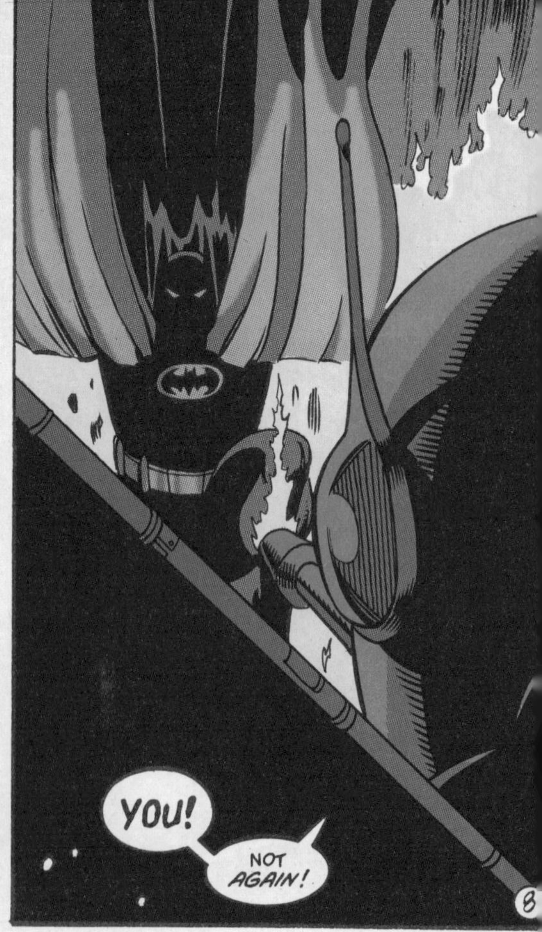
YOU!
NOT AGAIN!

YOU'VE SPOILED ENOUGH OF MY FUN, BATMAN!
YOU'LL BURN FOR IT!
YOU'LL BURN UNTIL THERE'S NOTHING LEFT!
THE HEAT.
THE HEAT IS OVERWHELMING.
IT SAPS MY LAST RESERVE OF STRENGTH.
9

BUT I'M NOT BURNING.
FIFTEEN-LAYER NOMEX AND A REBREATHER SHIELD ME FROM THE WORST OF IT.
STILL THE HEAT REACHES ME, STEALS MY STAMINA.
DON'T HAVE ANY TO SPARE.
HAVE TO TAKE LYNNS BEFORE IT'S ALL GONE.
BEFORE ALL OF GOTHAM BURNS.

THIS IS GOING OUT LIVE, RIGHT?
UH...YES IT IS.
RATINGS PRETTY HEALTHY, CASSIE?
WE'RE HOLDING OUR OWN. IT'S MOSTLY RE-RUNS ON THE OTHER STATIONS RIGHT NOW.

GOOD. I WANT TO GET A LARGE AUDIENCE. I'M SURE WE'LL WIN THIS TIME SLOT, DON'T YOU THINK?
I'M RUH... REASONABLY CERTAIN.
GETTING EXPOSURE IS SO HARD THESE DAYS. SO MUCH COMPETITION.

AND DR. FLANDERS, WE'VE MET BEFORE, HAVEN'T WE?
YUH-- YES, EDDIE.
AND I SEE YOU'VE WRITTEN A LITTLE BOOK, "I'M SANE AND SO ARE YOU."
SANE AND SO ARE YOU
DR SIMPSON FLAND

WELL, YOU COULDN'T HAVE WRITTEN IT WITH ME IN MIND.
EXCUSE ME?

'CAUSE I'M NOT SANE AND I NEVER WILL BE.
ISN'T THAT RIGHT, DOC?

AND HERE'S ANOTHER ONE FOR THE FOLKS AT HOME...
WHAT BEGINS WITH A P ENDS IN E AND HAS THOUSANDS OF LETTERS IN IT?
11

COME ON, FOLKS, THAT'S AN EASY ONE. A DEAD GIVEAWAY.
HAS HE MADE ANY THREATS?
WELL, NOT EXACTLY...
GET REAL, MONTOYA. THE GUY'S WEARING A DOZEN STICKS OF TNT. HE'S A WALKING THREAT. AND AFTER LOSING TWENTY COPS AT THE FUNHOUSE, I AIN'T TAKING NO CHANCES.
JUST KEEP GOING LIKE THIS WAS A REGULAR SHOW. OUR HOSTAGE NEGOTIATION TEAM IS ON THE WAY.
OH-KAY.
THIS IS TAC TEAM TWO. WHO'S IN CHARGE DOWN THERE?
THIS IS BULLOCK. UNTIL FURTHER NOTICE I AM.
I GOT THE TARGET IN MY CROSSHAIRS. CAN I GET A GREEN LIGHT?
POLICE
NEGATIVE. THAT GUY DROPS THAT RELEASE DETONATOR AND WE'RE WALLPAPER.
LET'S NOT DO ANYTHING CRAZY UNTIL WE HAVE TO. AND WHILE YOU'RE WAITING...
12

"...TRY TO FIGURE OUT WHAT THIS NUTBAR'S TALKING ABOUT."
U.S. MAIL
OH, THIS IS SWEET, BONEY.
GOTTA HAND IT TO THAT RIDDLER CREEP. HE PLANS A GREAT SCORE.
YEAH. IF IT WASN'T FOR HIS HANG-UP WITH THE PUZZLES HE'D BE A GENIUS.
BUT I GUESS BEIN' CRAZY IS PART OF BEIN' A GENIUS.
MAN... BLANK MONEY ORDERS, STAMPS, CASH. GOTTA BE AT LEAST A MILL IN THERE, HUH?
SHUT UP, OKAY? I'M POURIN' THE SOUP.
GET YOUR BUTTS DOWN AN' COVER YER EARS. THIS IS GONNA BE LOUD.
13

TRY TO LAND AS SOFT AS I CAN. PADDING HELPS SOME.
BUT NOT ENOUGH.
UFF!
A SHRIEK REMINDS ME THAT WE'RE NOT ALONE HERE.
OTHER CREATURES PROWL THE DARK.
DEADLIEST MANKILLER OF THEM ALL, THIS LEOPARD DOESN'T NEED THE FIRE TO DRIVE IT TO A KILLING FRENZY.
HELMET SAVES MY SKULL FROM TWO-INCH FANGS.
HAHAHAHA!
CLAWS SLASH THROUGH THE NOMEX LIKE PAPER.
HE'LL BE SHREDDING MY GUTS IN A SECOND.

♪ All the animals in the zoo are jumping up and down on you! ♪
I'D MUCH RATHER YOU'D BURNED, BATMAN. BUT A FLYING RODENT BEING EATEN BY A CAT IS SO MUCH MORE...
...POETIC.
HAVE TO BREAK AWAY BEFORE THE OTHERS JOIN IN.
MEANT THE FIRE RETARDANT OPTION FOR FIREFLY.
KITTY DOESN'T LIKE HALON.
RUN FOR THE FENCE BEFORE THEY RECOVER.
IT'S A MILLION MILES AWAY.
15

FLAMEPROOF OUTFIT IS CUMBERSOME.
ADD THAT TO EXHAUSTION AND INJURIES AND I'M NOT EXACTLY AT THE TOP OF MY FORM.
STOP COMPLAINING.
KEEP MOVING.
YOUR PROBLEMS DON'T MATTER.
YOU DON'T MATTER.
ONLY GOTHAM MATTERS.
HUH?
16

NO!
NOOOOOO!
YOU CAN'T LEAVE ME LIKE THIS!
YOU CAN'T!
IT'S TOO CRUEL!
COULDN'T PULL HIM UP IF I WANTED TO. WANT TO QUESTION HIM ABOUT BANE. TOO TIRED.
JUST DON'T HAVE ANYTHING LEFT.
17

AW COME ON, FOLKS!
THESE ARE THE EASY ONES! YOU MEAN NOT ONE OF YOU DUMMIES IN THE AUDIENCE CAN EVEN TAKE A GUESS?
MISS RUDOLPHO, IS THIS THE BEST YOU CAN DO? I HATE TO NITPICK BUT YOUR AUDIENCE MEMBERS ARE SUBMORONS.
I SHOULD HAVE PICKED ANOTHER SHOW TO DEBUT MY CRIME ON. MAYBE ENRICO RIVOLI OR--
UNNH?
WHAH?
SSSSS
JUST SOME FAST-ACTING EPOXY TO KEEP THAT HAND FROM RELAXING.
YOU WOULDN'T WANT TO BOMB IN THE RATINGS, RIGHT?
YOU LITTLE...
POLICE
FREEZE IT RIGHT THERE, RIDDLER.
GET THE BOMB SQUAD IN HERE!
18

YOU PUNK KID, HE COULD HAVE BLOWN THIS WHOLE BUILDING INTO NEXT YEAR!
YOU DIDN'T THINK!
BATMAN AND I HAVE DEALT WITH HIM BEFORE. I JUST THOUGHT...

WE HAD THIS PSYCHO COVERED.
AND IF I KNOW THE BAT-FREAK LIKE I THINK I DO, HE'LL HAVE A FEW WORDS ON THE SUBJECT HIMSELF.
BUT...
YO, HARV...

THE BOMB'S A FAKE. JUST WOODEN CHAIR RAILS WRAPPED IN ELECTRIC TAPE.
HEY, WATCH THE ARM, OKAY?
THAT DON'T CHANGE A THING, KID. THAT WAS STILL--

...A BONEHEAD PLAY.
MAN, I HATE THAT.

MY GOD, HOW AM I GOING TO FOLLOW THIS SHOW? DO YOU HAVE ANY IDEAS, DR. FLANDERS?
YES.
A CHANGE IN CAREERS.

SO WHAT WAS WITH ALL THE CRAZY RIDDLES? WHERE'S THE SCORE YOU'RE PULLING DOWN?
FIGURE IT OUT FOR YOURSELF.
19

"MAYBE NEXT TIME I'LL TRY MULTIPLE CHOICE."
THIS IS SO SWEET, BONEY. I'M FEELING SO GOOD I THINK MAYBE WE SHOULD CUT RIDDLER IN ON A PIECE OF THIS.
US MAIL
MAYBE FROM YOUR SHARE, STAN.
LET ME GUESS...
...YOU MAILED OFF A NASTY NOTE TO SOMEONE AND NOW YOU REGRET IT. AND YOU ONLY WANTED TO BREAK IN TO GET IT BACK.
DID I SEE THAT ON THE BRADY BUNCH OR THE JEFFERSONS?
MAYBE BOTH.

OR MAYBE YOU'RE JUST REAL SERIOUS STAMP COLLECTORS.
US MAIL
US MAIL
TWENTY STAMPS $5.80
WHO ARE YOU? BATLADY?
I DON'T LIKE IT WHEN THEY ASK WHO I AM!
BATMAN'S NOT THE ONLY ROOFRAT IN TOWN.
UNGH!
BET NOBODY EVER ASKS WHO HE IS.
HE'D GET TIRED OF THAT REAL QUICK.
NAW...
HOTEL
21

"...HE PROBABLY DOESN'T GET TIRED."
IT'S OVER.
FOR TONIGHT ANYWAY.
FIREFIGHTERS ARE HERE. THE ONES THAT AREN'T OUT ON STRIKE ANYWAY. THEY HAVE IT ALL IN HAND.
EIGHT DOWN. FIREFLY. ZSASZ. FILM FREAK. THE HATTER. CAVALIER. AMYGDALA. STIRK. POISON IVY.
MOSTLY SECOND-STRINGERS AND THEY NEARLY TOOK ME OUT.
THE REALLY DANGEROUS ONES ARE STILL ON THE STREET. SCARECROW. RIDDLER. JOKER.
HOW CAN I STAND AGAINST THEM WHEN I CAN'T EVEN STAND UP?
WHO WILL STAND BETWEEN GOTHAM AND BANE?
22

Gotham is a sea of chaos. Batman is drowning in it. Trapped by the Joker and the Scarecrow in a flooding Gotham Tunnel, the Dark Knight must save helpless Mayor Krol. Helpless...like Jason Todd, the previous Robin murdered by the Joker. The memory of Jason haunts the Batman... And so does Bane...
KNIGHTFALL
9
BATMAN 496 by Moench, Aparo, and Rubinstein
DC

DIE LAUGHING
SCORCHED AND SHREDDED, MAYBE A BROKEN RIB, ENERGY SAPPED... NEVER FELT SO WEAK, SO FOUL...
... BUT I'M NOT DEAD YET...
... AND THE MEDIA VULTURES CAN FEED ON SOME COLDER CARCASS.
BATMAN CREATED BY BOB KANE
DOUG MOENCH WRITER
JIM APARO PENCILLER
JOSEF RUBINSTEIN INKER
ADRIENNE ROY COLORIST
RICHARD STARKINGS LETTERER
JORDAN B. GORFINKEL ASSISTANT EDITOR
DENNIS O'NEIL EDITOR

AND SO, THIS IS GINA SCOVALL FOR GOTHAM-EYE NEWS -- AND THERE YOU HAVE THE STORY FROM THE ZOO.
FIREFIGHTERS HAVE THE VARIOUS BLAZES UNDER CONTROL, AND THE BATMAN IS ONCE AGAIN TRIUMPHANT--
--ALTHOUGH, AS USUAL, UN-AVAILABLE FOR AN INTERVIEW, AND REPORTEDLY MUCH THE WORSE FOR WEAR AFTER HIS BATTLE WITH THE FIREFLY.
THAT'S IT! OUR NEXT 'PHONE CALL!
KORN KURLS
KOLA
PRETZEL
BURGER

WHAT ARE YOU JABBERING ABOUT, JOKER? WHAT'S OUR NEXT 'PHONE CALL?
DIDN'T YOU HEAR, SCARECROW? BATS MAY BE DEAD ON HIS FEET...
... IN PERFECT POSITION TO BECOME DEAD ON HIS BACK!
HAHAHAHA
KOLA

AND YOU WANT TO USE THE GOOD MAYOR'S NEXT FEAR-GAS 'PHONE CALL TO LURE THE BATMAN INTO A TRAP.
PRECISELY.
NO WAY.

WHAT DO YOU MEAN, "NO WAY"?!
I MEAN, IT'S TOO SMALL, JOKER.
OTATO CHIPS
KOLA
WHEN WE COMBINED FORCES, WE AGREED TO DESTROY THE WHOLE CITY -- NOT JUST ONE MAN.

BUT THE CITY, YOU STRAW-STUFFED SIMPLETON, IS HIS -- AND ONCE WE TAKE HIM OUT, GOTHAM BECOMES OURS!
BESIDES, WE'VE GOT TO DO IT, FOR THE NOVELTY ALONE -- I'VE NEVER KILLED BATS BEFORE...
NATIONAL
CHIPS

GOT HIS SNOT-SNIVELING PARTNER ONCE...
... ALTHOUGH HE SEEMS TO BE BACK SOMEHOW...

SNAP OUT OF IT, YOU CLOWN!
I DECIDE HOW WE USE THIS FEAR-GAS, AND I SAID NO WAY!
Oh...
YOU DID, DID YOU?

BLSH
NATIONAL
POTATO

BAD MOVE...
... WHEN I COULD SQUISH THIS ANY TIME I WANT.

YOUR FEAR-GAS?!
I'M LOOKING FORWARD TO IT!
HAHAH HAH
3

NEW SUIT BUT NO SLEEP.
NO TIME -- KROL'S BEEN ABDUCTED BY THE JOKER -- BY JASON'S KILLER
VRAOOW
GOT TO LOOK FOR CLUES...
...IN THE MAYOR'S MANSION.
YOU... YOU WANT ME TO J-JUST GO IN THERE? I MEAN, AFTER WHAT HAPPENED AT THE AMUSEMENT PARK?
DO I DUST FOR FINGERPRINTS BEFORE OR AFTER I GET BLOWN TO RED MIST?
MONTOYA, YOU CAN STAND HERE AN' BASK IN THE GLOW O' THESE HEARTS O' FIRE --
-- OR YOU CAN COVER ME.
NO TIME TO WAIT ON THE BOMB SQUAD.
I'M GOIN' IN.

BASH

THUNG

PLACE IS RIGGED...

...AN' I TRIPPED IT.

TOO LATE TO GET AT THE CLUES...

JUST ENOUGH TIME --

UHNFF!!

--TO SAVE A CHINA SHOP BULL.

5

BWHOOOOM
BULLOCK!
YOU COULD HAVE WAITED.
"THE TRAP I DON'T MIND -- IT'S THE FACT THAT WE'LL BE IN IT."
"WE NEED BAIT, DON'T WE? AND IF KROL'S THE BAIT, WE'RE KROL'S KEEPERS, AREN'T WE?"
YES, BUT --
RELAX! I STOLE THE PLANS TO THIS TUNNEL FOR AN OLD ANTHRAX LAUGHING GAS CAPER -- MEMORIZED ALL THE ESCAPE DRAINS YEARS AGO!

TWO-FIFTY.
GOTHAM GAZETTE
MYSTERY

SETTLE FOR ONE?
WHAT THE--

HAHAHAHAHAHAHAHAHA

YECH

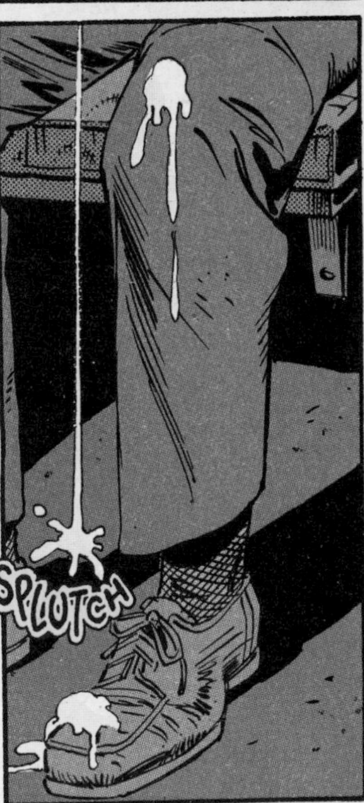
SPLUTCH

BAOOM
GOTH
TOLL
7

SKREEE
HONK
HAHAHA HAHAHA
HAHAHA
GIGGLY FREEZE ICES
WE'RE ON A SHORT FUSE, SCARE-CROW...
GO GO! GO!
GIGGLY FREEZE ICES
HALT! TRANSIT POLICE! HALT AND--
GIGGLY FREEZE ICES
POLICE
POLICE
BTOUM
8

HEY! WHAT WAS THAT NOISE? WHAT HAPPENED TO THE VEHICLE FLOW?!
WHAT THE DEVIL'S GOIN' ON OUT--

AHGK!
BRAM
BRAM
BRAM

THE LAST OF THE PRE-BLOCKADE VEHICLES SHOULD BE NEARING THE OTHER END OF THE TUNNEL BY NOW...

HEAT-SEEKER...
ZOOSH

"...HOTTEST ENGINE...

"...WINS!"
9

BUKDOOM
SKREEEE

SHMM

GOING SMOOTHLY SO FAR, JOKER... BUT ARE YOU SURE YOU KNOW A GOOD ESCAPE ROUTE?
HEY DO COBRA- KISS CARE- FULLY?
C-COBRAS?! .... N-NO......

...NO MORE Suh- SNAKES -- PLEASE...
THAT'S RIGHT, MISTER MAYOR, YOU DON'T LIKE SNAKES, DO YOU..? ALL THOSE VENOM-LOADED CURVED FANGS AND FLICKERING FORKED TONGUES...
SHKSH
BUT I'M AFRAID -- ALTHOUGH NOT AS AFRAID AS YOU -- THAT THE COBRAS ARE ALREADY ON THE MARCH, AND THE ONLY WAY FOR YOU TO STOP THE SLITHER...

...IS TO REACH OUT AND TOUCH THE POLICE COMMISSIONER.
HAHAH

BULLOCK, WHAT HAP--
THE BATMAN HAPPENED, MONTOYA--KNOCKED ME RIGHT OUTTA DEATH'S DOOR.
THE BATMAN? BUT... HE'S GONE!
'COURSE HE'S GONE...

AIN'T GONNA FIND NO CLUES IN THERE NOW.
ANY OTHER PLACES I'M BURNIN', MONTOYA? OR DID I PUT 'EM ALL OU--

=KSSS= TOLL BOOTH EXPLOSION =KSSS= HARBORSIDE ENTRANCE TO GOTHAM RIVER TUNNEL =KSSS=
POLICE
POLICE

YES, THIS IS COMMISSIONER GORDON, BUT IF YOU'RE REALLY MAYOR KROL, YOU'LL HAVE TO PROVE IT BY--
OUR... OUR PRIVATE TALKS, GORDON...

...ABOUT... ABOUT CALLING OUT THE NATIONAL GUARD? I... I THINK IT'S TIME... AND SUH-SEND THEM TO... THE GOTHAM RIVER TUNNEL.
...B-BEFORE THE SER--

--PENTS GET ME...
KLIK
PERFECT!
11

DID WE GET THE TRACE?!

CLAK
SKSH

-SKSS- THIS IS GORDON -- EMERGENCY OVERRIDE -SKSS- WE'VE JUST TRACED A PHONE CALL FROM MAYOR KROL AT A SERVICE BOOTH INSIDE GOTHAM RIVER TUNNEL -SKSS-

ALL UNITS CONVERGE ON THE TUNNEL -- BOTH ENDS -- BAYSIDE AND CENTER CITY -SKSS-
THIS'S BULLOCK, COMMISH -- HALF THE UNITS ARE ALREADY ON THEIR WAY -- RESPONDIN' TO THE EXPLOSIONS...

-SKSS- WE'LL MEET YA THERE... -SKSS-
BANE -- IT'S BEEN BANE FROM THE BEGINNING -- BUT HE'S USING THE JOKER AGAIN...

--TRAFFIC NOW ACKED UP FOR SIX ILES ON THE BAY IDE OF THE TUNNEL, S POLICE TRY TO ETERMINE THE AUSE OF THE MULTIPLE EXPLOSIONS...
WGOTV
NOT BAD, EH, BANE?

I ADMIT, BIRD, THAT THE JOKER AND THE SCARE-CROW DO COMBINE WELL FOR CHAOS.
WITH MORE DISCIPLINE, THEY COULD TAKE THE CITY.

BUT YOU STILL FIGURE THE BATMAN WILL STOP THEM?
HE'D BETTER -- BECAUSE ONCE HE GETS THROUGH THAT TUNNEL...
... HE RUNS OUR GAUNT-LET.

SO WHADDA WE DO, COMMISH? WE CAN'T JUST RUSH IN THERE--
--NOT AFTER LOSIN' A WHOLE TACTICAL TEAM IN THAT FUN-HOUSE...
I'M AWARE OF THAT, SERGEANT BULLOCK, BUT IF MAYOR KROL REALLY IS IN THE TUNNEL--
I'LL FIND HIM
13

AND I'LL BRING HIM OUT.

YOU REALIZE IT'S PROBABLY JUST ANOTHER TRAP...

A TRAP, GORDON, THAT COULD END THE MAYOR'S LIFE!

BUT--
JUST HOLD TIGHT, GORDON.
I'VE BEEN IN TRAPS BEFORE.
--FRESH RUMORS OF THE BATMAN'S PRESENCE ON THE SCENE...
AND I'M STUCK HERE IN THE NOWHERE CAVE...
EASY, TIMOTHY...

AT LEAST YOU STOPPED THE RIDDLER.
YEAH, AND WHEN BAT MAN FINDS OUT HOW, I'VE REALLY HAD IT.
Nmm, THERE IS THAT, ISN'T THERE?

"... IF THE MASTER EVER RETURNS HOME, THAT IS."
EXHAUSTED... EVERY STEP UPHILL... BUT I CAN'T REST, CAN'T FALTER...
...NOT WITH THE JOKER JUST AHEAD -- AND BEYOND HIM, BANE.
BATS'LL BE HERE SOON, SCARECROW -- GO OUT AND STAND WATCH.
I'LL TAKE CARE OF TAUNTING KROL.
GETTING SPACY NOW... HEAD SWIMMING... HARSH TANG OF BRIM-STONE...
BUT THERE -- JUST UP THE TUNNEL...
THE SCARECROW?
"I'LL TAKE CARE OF TAUNTING KROL -- WHILE YOU GO DO THE DIRTY WORK."
PFAH! IF ONLY MY FEAR-GAS WORKED ON THAT GRINNING JACKANAPE, I'D--
SWUD
UNFF!
SKSH
GAS--!
15

ROBIN! HE'S KILLING ROBIN!
NO -- NOT REAL -- JASON'S ALREADY DEAD -- JUST VISIONS... FROM THE GAS...
GOT TO FIGHT THROUGH THE VISIONS, AND --
-- GET RID OF THE GAS.
CHAT
BUT... JASON...
KTUNK
... JASON IS...
...DEAD.

SNAKES, MAYOR KROL, SERPENTS! VIPERS! VENOM AND FANGS!
HSSSS! RATTLERS!
HAHAHA
KRESH
Whuh--?
JUST A BOY GOOD AT HEART, MORE BRAVE THAN A MAN...
...TOO BRAVE TO BECOME A MAN.
KRISH
JASON...
TODD.
JUST A BOY, HIS PARENTS FELLED IN BLOOD, HIS OWN LIFE RIPPED AND TORN FROM THE WORLD HE PROTECTED.
JASON TODD!
JUST A BOY, BUT NEVER TO BREATHE, SPEAK, OR MOVE AGAIN.
JASON TODD!
17

JUST A BOY, BUT FAR TOO BRAVE TO FACE THE STARK, LURID MADNESS OF A GRINNING KILLER.
JASON!
KLUNCH
JUST A BOY-- DEAD -- BUT TO HIS KILLER, NOTHING MORE THAN A SICK JOKE!
SWAK
SHOK
CHOOF
SHUMP
CHUD

JUST A BOY -- BUT FOREVER GONE.
JASON!!!
SWOKK
SPLAM
19

G-GAS MADE HIM SEE... HIS GREATEST FEAR... BUT ONLY MADE HIM... MAD...
M-MISSILE... LAUNCHER...

USE IT, SCARE-CROW...
B-BLAST HIM TO GUANO.

WOOSH

KROOM

THE TUNNEL -- STARTING TO GIVE WAY -- AND WITH THE RIVER UP ABOVE --
KKKKKKK
G-GOT TO... GET OUT OF HERE, JOKER...
L-LOOKS LIKE IT WON'T HOLD FOR L-LONG, BATS... SO YOU'D BETTER M-MAKE YOUR CHOICE--
--STOP US... OR SAVE YOUR 'PHONE-PHREAK MAYOR!
HE'S RIGHT -- I CAN'T DO BOTH, NOT IN THIS CONDITION...
... WHICH LEAVES NO CHOICE AT ALL.
NO WAY I LET HIM KILL ANOTHER...
I'VE GOT TO SAVE KROL.
COME ON, YOU JAPING FOOL! THERE'S NO TIME TO WATCH--!
YOU'VE GOT TO GUIDE US TO THE ESCAPE TUNNELS!
21

K KKK KKK
BROOSH

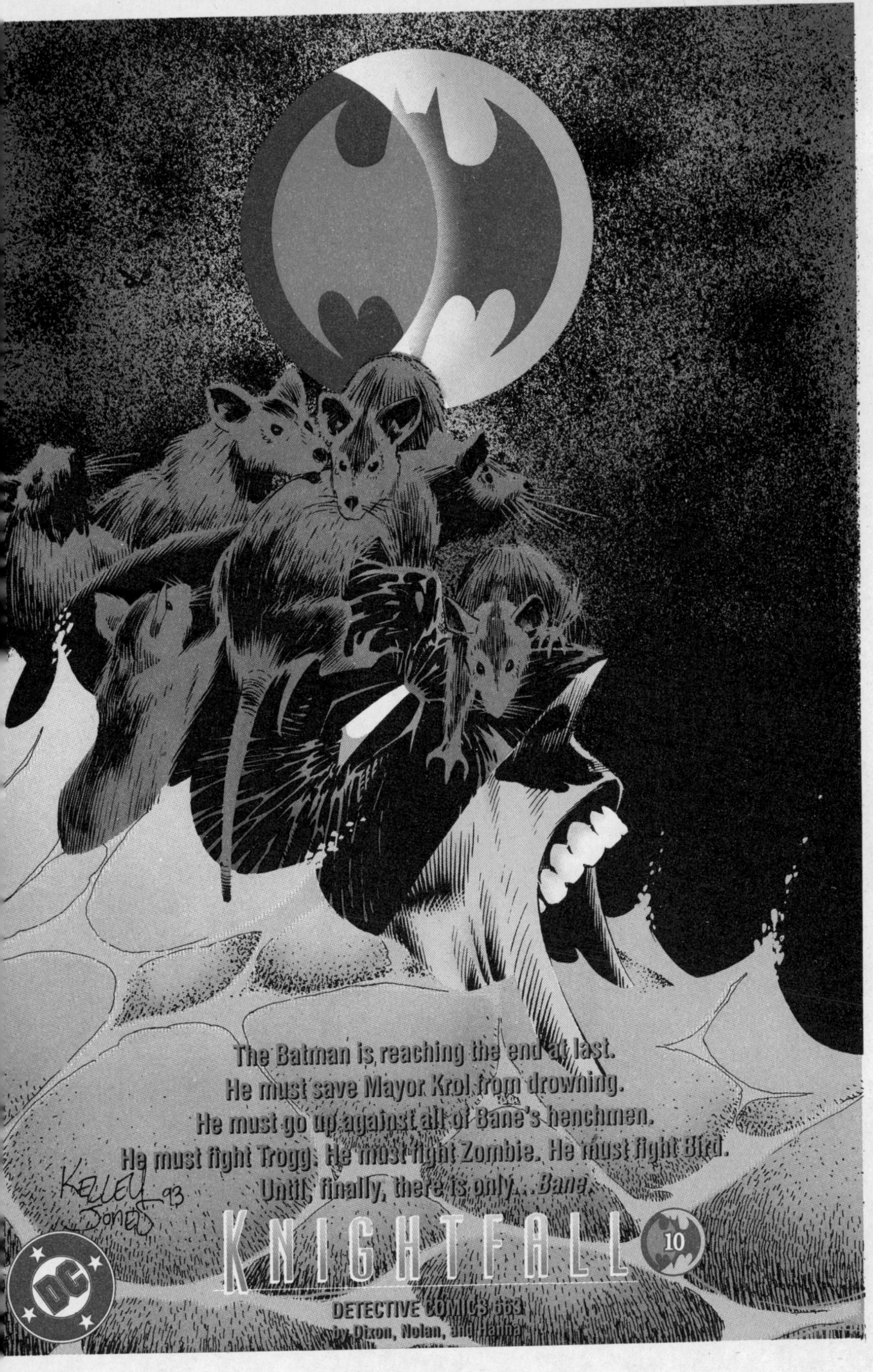

The Batman is reaching the end at last.
He must save Mayor Krol from drowning.
He must go up against all of Bane's henchmen.
He must fight Trogg. He must fight Zombie. He must fight Bird.
Until, finally, there is only... *Bane.*
Kelley Jones '93
KNIGHTFALL
10
DC
DETECTIVE COMICS 663
by Dixon, Nolan, and Hanna

NO REST FOR THE WICKED
RESCUE OF THE MAYOR WAS A TRAP JUST AS I SUSPECTED.
BUT WHAT CHOICE DID I HAVE?
JOKER'S PROBABLY GIGGLING HIMSELF SICK RIGHT NOW.
MAYBE HE'LL LAUGH HIMSELF TO DEATH.
CHUCK DIXON writer
GRAHAM NOLAN penciller
SCOTT HANNA inker
ADRIENNE ROY colorist
JOHN COSTANZA letterer
SCOTT PETERSON and DENNIS O'NEIL editors
BATMAN created by BOB KANE

ONE CHANCE TO GRAB A HANDHOLD AS THE WHOLE RIVER TRIES TO SWEEP US AWAY.
I MAKE IT. BUT HOW LONG CAN I HOLD?
AT LEAST SCARECROW'S FEAR GAS IS WEARING OFF.
KROL'S TRYING TO HELP. BUT HE'S IN SORRY SHAPE.
LIKE I'VE GOT ROOM TO TALK.
CAN YOU HOLD ON, MAYOR?
I... I CAN HOLD...
I SHOUT TO BE HEARD. THE NOISE OF THE WATER IS DEAFENING.
THE RIVER WILL FILL THE TUNNEL IN MOMENTS. THE ONLY WAY OUT IS *BELOW* THE WATERLINE.
WHUH-WHAT?
YOU JUST HOLD ON, MAYOR. I'LL BE BACK.
I'LL BE HERE.
2

KROL SOUNDS SCARED.
HE'S NOT REALLY A WEAK MAN. HE'S A FAIRLY STRONG ONE PUSHED BEYOND HIS LIMITS.
ALL MEN HAVE LIMITS. THEY LEARN WHAT THEY ARE AND THEN LEARN NOT TO EXCEED THEM.
I IGNORE MINE.
THIS IS WHAT I'M LOOKING FOR. THE LAST CHANCE FOR THE MAYOR AND ME.
3

THANK GOD!
WE HAVE TO SWIM DOWN TO THE TUNNEL WALKWAY. IT'S ABOUT THIRTY FEET BELOW US.
CAN YOU DO IT?
I DON'T KNOW. I'M SO TIRED. IT'S ALL I CAN DO TO HANG ON TO...
I DIDN'T THINK SO. A SHOT OF VER-SED RENDERS HIM UNCONSCIOUS.
THHHH...
THIS WAY HE CAN'T PANIC. THE CAPE WILL HOLD A FEW MINUTES OF AIR AROUND HIM.
IF I FAIL THEN HE'LL JUST NEVER WAKE UP.
REBREATHER'S EXHAUSTED. DOWN TO THE FOUR MINUTES OF AIR I CAN HOLD IN MY LUNGS.

SERVICE TUNNEL.
MAY LEAD TO THE RIVERBANK.

MAY LEAD NOWHERE.
TUNNEL BEHIND US IS FULL.

SERVICE CONDUIT WILL FILL TO RIVERLEVEL IN NO TIME.
THEN IT'S OVER.

END OF THE LINE. WATER'S FILLING THE TUNNEL.

AIR PRESSURE BUILDING.
LIKE MY HEAD IS BEING PRESSED BETWEEN TWO GIANT HANDS.
5

HATCH RUSTED SHUT. MAYBE BLOCKED.
STOP COMPLAINING AND GET THE JOB DONE.
IT CAN'T END LIKE THIS.
NOT AT THE HAND OF THE JOKER.
NO. NOT THE JOKER.
BANE.
HE ENGINEERED THIS.
HE'S THE ONE WHO WANTS ME DEAD.
SKRIK SKRIK
BANE.
6

I WON'T DIE AND LEAVE THE CITY AT HIS MERCY.
HE'LL NEVER HAVE GOTHAM.
KROL'S STILL ALIVE.
BUT IN SHOCK.
I CAN HEAR HARBOR SOUNDS.
DAMN IT. WHAT CAN WE DO BUT WATCH?
RIVER COPS ARE CIRCLING THE AREA AROUND THE BLAST, COMMISSIONER.
I CAN SMELL THE IRON-TINGED AIR OF THE CITY.
WHAT'S THE POINT, MONTOYA? IF HIZZONER WAS DOWN IN THAT TUNNEL WHEN IT BLEW, HE'S RETIRED FROM OFFICE PERMANENT.
7

BULLOCK, OF ALL THE CALLOUS AND BRUTAL THINGS I'VE HEARD COME OUT OF THAT MOUTH OF YOURS...
WHAT'D I SAY?
COMMISSIONER! LOOK DOWN THERE!
IT'S MAYOR KROL!
GET THE PARAMEDICS OVER HERE! FAST!
DEAR GOD...I...I...
IT'S ALL RIGHT, YOUR HONOR. YOU'RE SAFE NOW.
HOW DID YOU ESCAPE THE TUNNEL, MAYOR? WE JUST ABOUT GAVE YOU UP.
HE NEVER GAVE UP.
WHO, MAYOR? WHO NEVER GAVE UP?
THE BATMAN...
HE DOESN'T KNOW WHAT IT MEANS TO SURRENDER.

VISION BLURRING. LIGHT-HEADED. STARTING TO GET THE SHAKES.
USED MYSELF UP OPENING THAT HATCH.
HAVE TO GET TO SHELTER... TO DARKNESS WHILE I STILL HAVE SOMETHING LEFT.
JUST A LITTLE REST AND I'LL BE FINE.
CAN'T LET ANYONE CATCH ME LIKE THIS.
PUT A LOT OF THEM AWAY.
BUT STILL TOO MANY ENEMIES LOOSE ON THE STREETS.
9

IMPOUND OFFICE
ALL THE MOST DANGEROUS ONES ARE STILL FREE.
EXCUSE US, ME LAD. I'VE SOME PROPERTY I NEED TO COLLECT.
WHUZZ? WHUH?

OKAY, OKAY. YOU GOT A CLAIM NUMBER AND COURT DATE? I'LL GO GET IT FOR YOU.
THAT I DO, THAT I DO, ME BOYO.
CAN THE STUPID BROGUE AND HAND OVER THE PAPERWORK, WISEGUY.

SURE'N I CAN DO JUST THAT.
BLAM
BLAM
BLAM
UGH!

SPLANG!
BLAM!

IS HE HERE?
SHHH!
WELL, WHERE IS HE?

SO THAT'S HIM.
THAT'S THE MIGHTY SCARFACE.

"AW, HE DON'T LOOK SO TOUGH."
JUST A FEW MOMENTS' REST AND THEN BACK TO THE STREETS.
A SOUND.
IT STARTLES THE BIRDS.
A FALCON'S CRY.
ROBIN SAID ONE OF BANE'S MEN IS A FALCONER.
COULD THEY BE...?
11

WHY IS BANE OBSESSED WITH YOU?
IT MAKES NO SENSE. IT NEVER HAS.
HIDING FROM US.
HIDING LIKE THE CRAVEN RODENT THAT YOU PRETEND TO BE.
NO MATCH FOR HIM IN THIS CONDITION.
HAVE TO RELY ON MY ARSENAL.
TROGG WILL SHOW HIM THAT YOU ARE BENEATH HIS CONSIDERATION.
WHEN I CRUSH THE LIFE FROM YOU!
A WET SNAP IN MY SIDE. HAS TO BE A RIB.

UNNH!
YOU KNOW NOTHING OF TROGG!
YOU THINK A STING LIKE THAT WILL MAKE ME RELEASE YOU?
NOT ENTIRELY.
JUST A BIT...
MY OWN RECIPE OF CS GAS.
UNCONTROLLABLE NAUSEA AND DIS-ORIENTATION.
13

TROGG LAUGHED IN A LUNGFUL.
MY NEXT BREATH REMINDS ME OF THE BROKEN RIB.
A LANCE OF FIRE BURNS.
ROBIN SAID THERE WERE THREE MEN WITH BANE.
AM I RUNNING SOME KIND OF GAUNTLET?
HEAD SWIMMING.
PAIN IN MY SIDE GETTING SHARPER.
ISOLATE THE PAIN. LOCK IT AWAY.
PUT IN A TINY BOX IN A CORNER OF MY MIND.
SHHNK!
I'M THE CITY'S ONLY HOPE.

I'M ALL THAT STANDS BETWEEN THESE MONSTERS AND GOTHAM.
IT TAKES AN EXCELLENT EYE TO MISS THAT ACCURATELY.
I JUST WANTED YOU TO KNOW THAT I DO NOT RELY ON BRUTE STRENGTH.
THIS ONE MUST BE ZOMBIE.
SO IT'S ANOTHER TEST.
LIKE BREAKING THE INMATES OUT OF ARKHAM.
ALL TO TEST MY ABILITIES AND ENDURANCE.
AS THOUGH BANE WERE STUDYING ME.
TO WHAT END?
15

WHY NOT JUST FACE ME?
WEGM

UH?
DESPITE THE PAIN...
...DESPITE THE EXHAUSTION...
...THAT FELT GOOD.
17

KREEEEE
THE FALCONER.
KREEE-EEEE

THE LAST ONE BEFORE BANE,

HE COULD MEAN FOR THE FALCON TO FINISH ME.

OR I COULD BE RUN INTO A TRAP.
SO YOU FOUND YOUR WAY HERE.
DON'T LOOK SO BIG AND SCARY NOW, HUH?

OU'RE SUPPOSED TO BE
UCH A HOTSHOT. BANE
ELIEVES YOU ARE,
NYWAY. I USED TO,
TOO.
NOW I THINK YOU'RE
ALL BLUFF, MASKED
MAN.
THE CAPE,
THE BOGEY MAN
ACT. THEY'RE
JUST THAT--
AN
ACT!
NOBODY CAN HEAR YOU.
GO AHEAD--
SCREAM.
LET ME HEAR
HOW MUCH IT
HURTS, TOUGH
GUY.
I TOLD
BANE YOU
RAN GOTHAM.
NOT FOR
LONG,
HUH?
14

BANE...
BANE...
BANE.
BANE!
WHO IS HE? WHAT DOES HE WANT? ANSWER ME!
HE SAID I WOULD SCREAM HIS NAME.

ALL A BLUR FROM HERE.
SHADOWS AND DARK.
DON'T REMEMBER GETTING TO THE CAR.
RECALL RIDE HOME ONLY IN SNATCHES.
HOME.
CAN'T WEAR COSTUME UPSTAIRS. PROMISED ALFRED.

WHERE IS ALFRED?
I COULD HAVE PUT UP WITH HIS SARCASM IN EXCHANGE FOR SOME HELP UP THE STAIRS.

ALFRED?
I LEFT HIM ALIVE. IT IS NOT YOUR UNDERLINGS I WANT...
THE VOICE.
21

IT'S HIM.
...IT IS YOU.

BANE.
Batman is going where he has never gone before...
Away.
KNIGHTFALL
11
DC
BATMAN 497 by Moench, Aparo and Giordano

FEEL SO BAD, I WANT TO DIE...
...AND NOW...
...HE'S HERE, IN WAYNE MANOR...
BANE.
...READY AND WILLING TO GRANT MY WISH.
THE BROKEN BAT
DOUG MOENCH WRITER
JIM APARO ARTIST
DICK GIORDANO INKER
ADRIENNE ROY COLORIST
RICHARD STARKINGS LETTERER
JORDAN B. GORFINKEL ASST. EDITOR
DENNIS O'NEIL EDITOR
BATMAN CREATED by BOB KANE

YOU... YOU KNOW WHO I --
YOU COULD BE NO ONE ELSE.
THIS "BRUCE WAYNE" IS NOTHING BUT A MASK -- AND ONE WHICH NO LONGER SERVES ANY PURPOSE...
...ALTHOUGH MY MASK --
TEK
FSHHH
-- STILL DOES.
A DIRECT FEED THROUGH THE HELMET -- STRAIGHT INTO MY BRAIN AND BLOODSTREAM -- BURNING MY VEINS WITH A VERY SPECIAL POTION...
THE VENOM DERIVATIVE.

VENOM, YES -- YOU FOUND SOME, NO DOUBT, PUMPED INTO THE RIDDLER.
AND YOU ARE... FAMILIAR WITH VENOM?
YES.
THEN YOU KNOW WHAT IT CAN DO?
ALL TOO WELL.
YOU THINK SO? I THINK NOT.
I WAS ONCE MADE A GUINEA PIG FOR AN EXPERI-MENTAL "IMPROVED CONCENTRATE" OF VENOM.
TRUST ME, NO MATTER WHAT YOUR PRIOR EXPERIENCE, YOU KNOW NOTHING OF MY VENOM.
THE SHEER STRENGTH AND FEROCITY NOW COURSING THROUGH ME IS ENOUGH TO BREAK A MAN -- ANY MAN -- LIKE A DEAD STICK.
HOW DID YOU KNOW --
I'VE KNOWN YOU SINCE I LIVED IN THE HELL OF A DARK HOLE THOUSANDS OF MILES FROM HERE.
I'VE KNOWN YOU IN MY DREAMS.
3

AND I ESCAPED FROM THAT HELL -- ESCAPED FROM MY DREAMS -- FOR ONE REASON ONLY.
TO FIND YOU -- AND TO BREAK YOU.
WHY? WHAT HAS IT ALL BEEN ABOUT? FREEING THE INMATES FROM ARKHAM, WATCHING ME DEAL WITH THEM, WATCHING THEM WEAR ME DOWN... WAS IT ALL JUST TO LEARN ABOUT ME? TO WEAKEN ME?
THERE MUST BE MORE TO IT -- BUT WHAT?
GOTHAM -- THE ULTIMATE PRIZE.
YOU HAVE IT.
I WANT IT.

AND ALL THE DEATHS... ALL THE WASTED LIVES... IT'S BEEN NOTHING BUT THAT?
YOU'D KILL JUST TO "RULE" THIS CITY? JUST FOR--

I'D KILL FOR ANY-THING.
I'D KILL TO SILENCE A GRATING VOICE.
TO DARKEN THE LIGHT IN EYES THAT DARED LOOK AT ME.

THEN WHILE YOU REVEL IN IT, BANE, I'M SICK OF DEATH -- SICK OF BLOOD -- SICK OF THE CHAOS AND HORROR YOU'VE BROUGHT TO GOTHAM --
--AND RIGHT INTO MY HOME.

I'VE SPENT MY LIFE FIGHTING YOUR KIND OF MADNESS AND EVIL --
--AND NOW THAT LIFELONG FIGHT HAS BROUGHT ME TO DEATH'S DOOR, MY OWN DOOR...

I WOULD NOT BE HERE WERE IT OTHERWISE.
I REALIZE THAT -- AND I REALIZE YOU MAY WELL BE THE SINGLE GREATEST SOURCE OF MADNESS AND EVIL I'VE EVER FACED...
EASILY.

AND IN THAT CASE...
...ONE MORE TIME.

BUT THIS TIME IS DIFFERENT.
5

THIS TIME IS --
THUNCH
--DOOMED.

PUSHING TOO HARD FOR TOO LONG...
KRESH
UHN

...FACING THE MADNESS OF TOO MANY MASKS...

...BEARING THE BRUNT OF TOO MUCH VIOLENCE...
S-SIR? ARE... ARE YOU--
G-GO, ALFRED...
GET OUT OF HERE BEFORE--

AGH-K!
SIR--
...TOO MUCH PAIN...

ALREADY BURNED DOWN AND OUT FROM ENDS AND EVERY ANGLE...
...BATTERED, BASHED AND SCARRED FROM A THOUSAND CUTS AND BLOWS...
...TOTTERING ON BRITTLE BONES AND LURCHING THROUGH VERTIGO FOR MONTHS NOW...
SIR--!
WUMP
...EARS BUZZING AND RINGING... EVERY-THING TOO BRIGHT AND GLITTERY...
...EVEN IN THE DARK...
7

TOO MUCH PUNISHMENT... OVERWHELMING ODDS...

PASSING BLOOD FOR WEEKS...
CHUMP
...RACING FOR DEATH MY WHOLE LIFE...

G-GOT TO... GET HELP...

EVERY MUSCLE SLUGGISH... SLUGGISH AND TREMBLING...

...ALL STRENGTH STRETCHED AND SAPPED, WASHED IN WEAKNESS...

KRUNCH
...MIRED IN A SLOW-MOTION PANIC OF HELPLESSNESS...
...AND THROUGH IT ALL, NO SLEEP, NO REST...
...EVEN WHEN MOVEMENT ITSELF WAS IMPOSSIBLE...
...NOTHING BUT THE MIND'S DESPERATE URGE TO GET OFF THE FLOOR AND STRIKE BACK.
CHFT
...EVEN WHEN EVERY UPHILL EFFORT IS WASTED AND FUTILE...
YOU ARE ALREADY BROKEN.
...REALITY ITSELF SMASHED AND SPLINTERED, LIKE THE RUDE DEATH OF AN IMPOSSIBLE DREAM...
9

...AWAKENING AGAIN AND AGAIN TO NOTHING BUT AGONY, RELENTLESS AND REPEATED...
SHOKK
AND THEN THE CROWNING HORROR OF SHATTERED ARKHAM...
...SPILLING ITS MAD GUTS INTO THE LONG DARK NIGHT OF HOPELESS HORROR.

T-TIM..!
A LEGION OF CRAZED KILLERS LOOSED ON GOTHAM... TOO MANY AND TOO MUCH TO FIGHT...
IT IS OVER.
YOU ARE NOTHING.
...THE TOLL TOO GREAT, PRIDE NO LONGER AN ASSET... ONLY PRELUDE TO A FALL...
KWUMP
...LEAVING ME DRAINED AND DEPLETED...
A DISAPPOINTMENT!
...UTTERLY EMPTY.
11

BUT STILL THEY LOOMED AND LUNGED FROM THE DARK...
...LAUGHING DEMONS WITH BAD INTENT...
...BEARING PAIN AND NOTHING MORE...
SHUMP
...CHIPPING AWAY AT WHATEVER WAS LEFT...
WUMP
...WEARING ME DOWN TOWARD NOTHING...
BRIIING
BRIIING
STILL NOT HOME...
...EVEN AT NIGHT.
DR. SHONDRA KINS
...AND NOWHERE.
THWOK
12

VERTIGO... WHIRLING OUT OF CONTROL NOW... TIME DISTORTED... IMAGES FLASHING...
...THEN AND NOW A CONFUSED BLUR...
ONE CENT UNITED STATES OF AMERICA
WHY DON'T YOU FIGHT?!
BAMP
...EVERY SHOCK AND CONCUSSION THE SAME...
...EACH DEVASTATING...
...AND ALL ADDING UP...
PRAK
...TO ONE LONG PLUNGE INTO HELL...
13

...NIGHTMARISH...
YOU'VE GOT NO SPINE!
...NEVER-ENDING...
WUBBASHT
...GARISH AND BIZARRE...
SWAP
THMP
...INSANITY TOO STARK TO SUFFER OR SURMOUNT.
ALL OF THEM... THEY ALL HAD A HAND IN IT...

...BUT IT WAS BANE'S BLOODY HAND BEHIND THEM, BEHIND IT ALL.
CHOOOF
BANE FROM THE BEGINNING-- AND BANE NOW, AT THE END.
KESSH
NO... CAN'T GIVE IN, NOT NOW, NO MATTER HOW HURT... CAN'T LET HIM WIN...
CAN'T SURRENDER TO THE BLESSED RELIEF... OF ENDING IT ALL.
JASON... ROBIN...
15

TIM--!

HELP, TIM--!
BAMP
BAMP
BAMP

TIMOTHY, THANK GOD! WE'VE GOT TO --
ALFRED! WHAT HAPPENED TO YOUR HEA--
NEVER MIND THAT, TIM!

THE MASTER NEEDS HELP, AND IT'S BAD! WE MUST GET JEAN PAUL AND --
WHAT?
KEEP YOUR VOICE DOWN, ALFRED, BEFORE YOU WAKE DAD.
HOW BAD?

I... I DON'T KNOW, LAD, BUT WE... WE MAY NEED...
... AN AMBULANCE.

I...
I'LL GET MY COSTUME.

HARSH TANG OF BRIMSTONE EXPANDING IN MY CHEST... EVERY BREATH HOT AND BITTER... BUT I CAN'T GIVE IN...
GOT TO TRY... EVEN WITH NO MORE SPRING IN MY STEP, NO BITE OF BOOT INTO GROUND...

...NO MORE POWER...
YOU HAVE NOTHING!
...NO MORE SPEED...

THUP

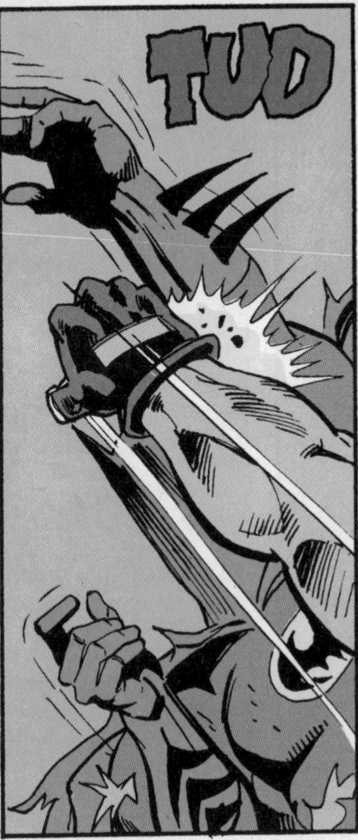
TUD

CHWOK
...NO MORE REFLEXES.
17

SKUTCH
AHRRR!
THAT'S... IT...

...GAVE MY ALL... LONG AGO...

...AND WHAT'S LEFT...
Ahn--!
...ISN'T ENOUGH...

...NOT WHEN I'VE ALREADY TAKEN MORE DAMAGE THAN ANY MAN CAN ENDURE...
...ALL IN A LOSING CAUSE.

...AND NOW... FEEL SO BAD... I WANT TO DIE...
BEG FOR MERCY!
SCREAM MY NAME!
G-GO... BACK TO...
...HELL.
AND I'M... DONE.
SWOK
19

I AM BANE -- AND I COULD KILL YOU...
... BUT DEATH WOULD ONLY END YOUR AGONY -- AND SILENCE YOUR SHAME.
INSTEAD, I WILL SIMPLY...
20

...BREAK YOU!
KRAKT
21

BROKEN...
DUFT
...AND DONE.